teach yourself®

powerpoint 2002

moira stephen

The **teach yourself** series does exactly what it says, and it works. For over 60 years, more than 40 million people have learnt over 750 subjects the **teach yourself** way, with impressive results.

be where you want to be with **teach yourself**

For UK orders: please contact Bookpoint Ltd., 130 Milton Park, Abingdon, Oxon OX14 4SB. Telephone: +44 (0)/1235 827720. Fax: +44 (0)/1235 400454. Lines are open 09.00–18.00, Monday to Saturday, with a 24-hour message answering service. You can also order through our website www.madaboutbooks.com.

For USA order enquiries: please contact McGraw-Hill Customer Services, PO Box 545, Blacklick, OH 43004-0545, USA. Telephone: 1-800-722-4726. Fax: 1-614-755-5645.

For Canada order enquiries: please contact McGraw-Hill Ryerson Ltd., 300 Water St, Whitby, Ontario L1N 9B6, Canada. Telephone: 905 430 5000. Fax: 905 430 5020.

Long renowned as the authoritative source for self-guided learning – with more than 30 million copies sold worldwide – the *Teach Yourself* series includes over 300 titles in the fields of languages, crafts, hobbies, business, computing and education.

British Library Cataloguing in Publication Data
A catalogue record for this title is available from The British Library.

Library of Congress Catalog Card Number: On file.

First published in UK 2003 by Hodder Headline Plc., 338 Euston Road, London, NW1 3BH.

First published in US 2003 by Contemporary Books, A Division of The McGraw-Hill Companies, 1 Prudential Plaza, 130 East Randolph Street, Chicago, Illinois 60601 USA.

Typeset by MacDesign, Southampton
Printed in Great Britain for Hodder & Stoughton Educational, a division of Hodder Headline Plc, 338 Euston Road, London NW1 3BH by Cox & Wyman Ltd., Reading, Berkshire.

Impression number 10 9 8 7 6 5 4 3 2

Year 2007 2006 2005 2004 2003

contents

01	**getting started**	**1**
1.1	Introducing PowerPoint	2
1.2	Hardware and software requirements	3
1.3	Installing PowerPoint 2002	4
1.4	PowerPoint objects	4
1.5	Starting PowerPoint	5
1.6	The PowerPoint Window	6
1.7	Menus	7
1.8	Help!	8
1.9	Help on the Internet	15
1.10	Exiting PowerPoint	16
02	**basic powerpoint skills**	**18**
2.1	New presentations	19
2.2	Saving a presentation	23
2.3	Closing and opening files	24
2.4	View options	25
2.5	Outline and Slides pane	26
2.6	Notes pane	27
2.7	Hide/Restore panes	28
2.8	Moving through the slides	28
03	**working with slides**	**30**
3.1	Adding and deleting slides	31
3.2	Moving or copying a slide	32

	3.3	Formatting text	33
	3.4	Paragraph formatting	34
	3.5	Rearranging the bullet points	36
	3.6	Changing a slide layout	40
	3.7	Changing the design template	40
	3.8	Comments	41
04	**drawing**		**43**
	4.1	The Drawing toolbar	44
	4.2	Text box tool	45
	4.3	Drawing tools	46
	4.4	AutoShapes	48
	4.5	Rotate and Flip	49
	4.6	Changing the order	50
	4.7	Group and UnGroup	51
	4.8	WordArt	52
05	**charts**		**54**
	5.1	Creating a chart	55
	5.2	Microsoft Graph	56
	5.3	Chart Type	59
	5.4	Chart objects	61
	5.5	Scale	63
	5.6	Combination charts	64
	5.7	Overlap and Gap Width	64
	5.8	Leaving Microsoft Graph	65
	5.9	Importing a chart from Excel	65
06	**organization charts and diagrams**		**68**
	6.1	Creating an organization chart	69
	6.2	Adding and deleting boxes	72
	6.3	Layout	73
	6.4	Animation	74
	6.5	Diagrams	77
	6.6	Working with Shapes	79
	6.7	AutoFormat	80

07	**tables, clip art and sound**	**82**
7.1	Tables	83
7.2	Clip art	86
7.3	Clip Organizer	87
7.4	Sound	93
08	**masters**	**95**
8.1	Slide Master	96
8.2	Headers and Footers	99
8.3	Handout Master	99
8.4	Notes Master	100
09	**slide show preparation**	**102**
9.1	Slide Sorter toolbar	103
9.2	Rehearse timings	104
9.3	Summary Slide	106
9.4	Speaker Notes	106
9.5	Transition	107
9.6	Animation	108
9.7	Set Up Show	110
9.8	Custom Show	112
10	**giving a slide show**	**115**
10.1	Slide Show	116
10.2	Blackout and whiteout	117
10.3	Meeting Minder	118
10.4	PowerPoint Show	121
11	**printing presentations**	**122**
11.1	Page setup	123
11.2	Printing slides	125
11.3	Print dialog box	128
12	**jumps and links**	**130**
12.1	Action buttons	131
12.2	Mixed slide orientation	133
12.3	Hyperlink from any object	134

13	**toolbars**	**136**
13.1	Showing and hiding toolbars	137
13.2	Moving toolbars	138
13.3	Editing existing toolbars	139
13.4	Reset toolbar	142
13.5	Creating a new toolbar	143
14	**powerpoint with other applications**	**144**
14.1	Linking vs embedding	145
14.2	Copy and paste	146
14.3	Copy and paste special	147
14.4	PowerPoint and Word	148
	taking it further	**150**
	index	**152**

getting started

In this chapter you will learn

- what you need to run PowerPoint 2002
- how to install the software
- how to start PowerPoint
- about the PowerPoint screen and its tools
- how to use the Help system

Aims of this chapter

This chapter will introduce you to PowerPoint. We will start with an overview of the package, and move on to consider the hardware and software specification required to run it. We then move on to look at how you install the package on your computer. PowerPoint objects, starting PowerPoint, the working environment, on-line Help system and exiting PowerPoint will also be discussed.

1.1 Introducing PowerPoint

PowerPoint is a presentation graphics package. If you have to make presentations, it can help make your life easier by giving you the tools you need to produce your own materials with little or no help from presentation graphics specialists.

You can use PowerPoint to produce:

Slides

Slides are the individual pages of your presentation. They may contain text, graphs, clip art, tables, drawings, animation, movies, music, shapes – and more!! PowerPoint will allow you to present your slides via a slide show on your computer, 35mm slides or overhead projector transparencies.

Speaker's Notes

A speaker's notes page accompanies each slide you create. Each notes page contains a small image of the slide plus any notes you type in. You can print the pages and use them to prompt you during your presentation.

Handouts

Handouts consist of smaller, printed versions of your slides that can be printed 1, 2, 3, 4, 6 or 9 slides to a page. They provide useful backup material for your audience and can easily be customized with your company name or logo.

Outline

A presentation Outline contains the slide titles and main text items, but neither art nor text added by using the text tool. The Outline gives a useful overview of your presentation's structure.

- A PowerPoint presentation is a collection of slides, with optional, but useful support materials, speaker's notes, handouts and an outline, all in one file.

1.2 Hardware and software requirements

The hardware and software specifications given are for Office XP. The recommended configuration is a PC with Windows 2000 or XP, a Pentium III Processor and 128 MB of RAM.

The minimum specification is:

Personal Computer	Pentium 133 MHz or higher processor
Operating System	Windows 98, Windows Me, Windows NT 4.0 with Service Pack 6 (SP6) or later, Windows 2000, or Windows XP.
RAM	Depends on the operating system used, plus 8MB for each office application in use at one time. **Windows 98**: 24 MB of RAM **Windows Me or NT**: 32 MB of RAM **Windows 2000 or XP**: 64 MB of RAM
Hard disk	Approximately 245 MB of hard disk space in total, with 115 MB on the hard disk where the operating system is installed.
CD-ROM Drive	The software is only supplied on CD
Monitor	Super VGA or higher-resolution
Mouse	Microsoft Mouse, IntelliMouse® or compatible pointing device

See **http://www.microsoft.com/uk/office/evaluation/sysreqs.asp** for full details of system requirements.

1.3 Installing PowerPoint 2002

PowerPoint is supplied in the following Office XP editions.

Standard: Word, Excel, Outlook and PowerPoint.

Professional: As Standard plus Access and FrontPage

Developer: As Professional plus Sharepoint Team Services, Developer tools.

Professional with Publisher: (only available pre-installed)

These instructions are for installing Microsoft Office.

1 Insert the CD into the CD drive
2 Follow the instructions on your screen

1.4 PowerPoint objects

In PowerPoint you work with *objects*. These may be:

- Text
- Drawings
- Graphs
- Organization charts
- Clip art
- Movies
- Sounds
- Tables

Clip art can enliven your text – a wide variety of images are supplied with PowerPoint.

- Annotated graphs can be produced very easily.
- Special text effects can be created using WordArt
- Tables are useful for statistics

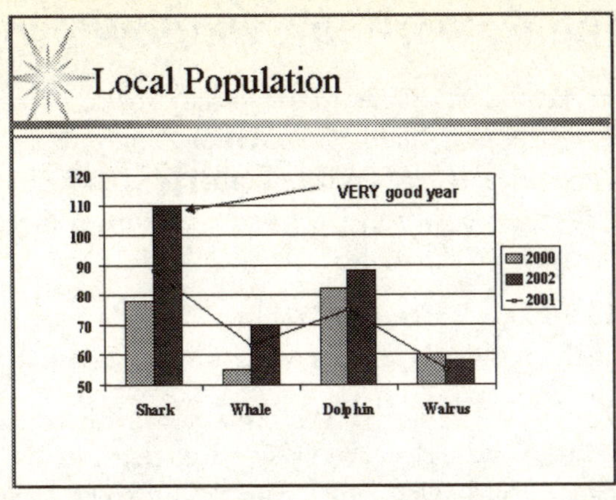

Organization charts are simple to create – once you've worked out the structure of your organization!

You'll learn how to create and manipulate these objects as you work with the package.

1.5 Starting PowerPoint

Starting through the Shortcut Bar:

- Click the PowerPoint tool

From the Start menu:

1 Click the **Start** button on the Task Bar

2 Point to **Programs**

3 Click **Microsoft PowerPoint**

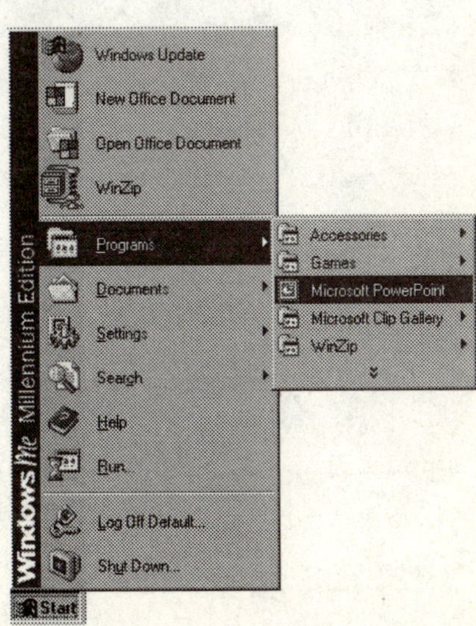

1.6 The PowerPoint window

Whichever method you prefer to use to start PowerPoint, you are presented with a new blank presentation, ready to start. The PowerPoint window is very similar to other Microsoft application windows. If you use Word, Excel or Access you will recognize some of the tools on the toolbars.

The Standard and Formatting toolbars usually appear along the top of the window. The Drawing toolbar is usually along the bottom of the window.

We'll take a tour of the PowerPoint screen, so that you know what the various areas are called. You'll find the different screen areas referred to by their 'proper' names in the on-line Help, throughout this book and in other publications on the package.

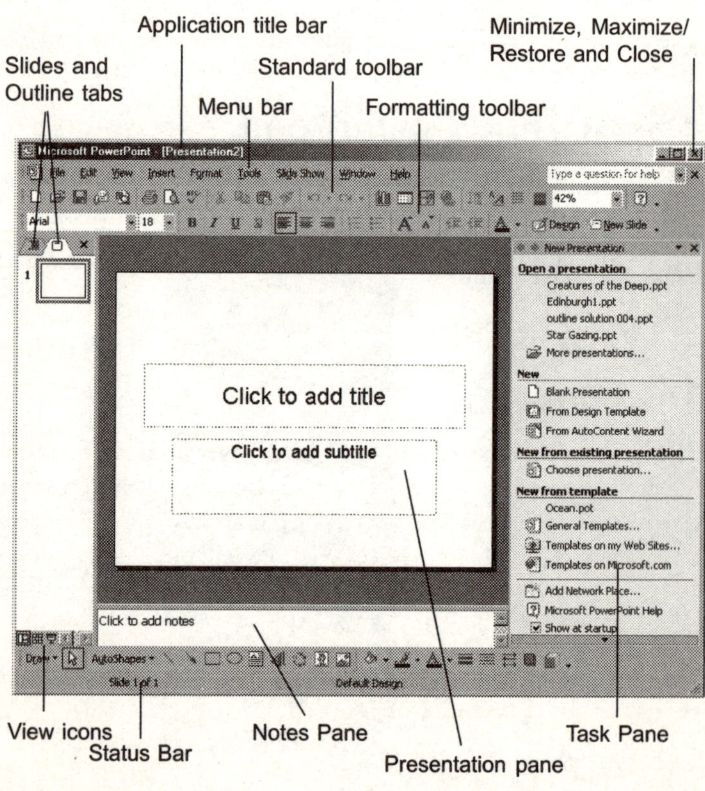

Menus and toolbars

Office XP applications personalize your menus and toolbars automatically. The items that you use most often are featured on your personalized toolbars or menus.

Once you start using PowerPoint, you'll find that the menu options most recently used will be displayed first when you open a menu (this is your personalized menu). You can expand the menus to reveal all commands (simply click on the down arrow that appears at the bottom of each menu). You may find that the menu automatically expands if you just wait once you've opened it. If you wish to modify the way that the menus work, open the **View** menu choose **Toolbars, Customize.** You can switch the **Show full menus after a short delay** option on or off on the **Options** tab.

The Standard and Formatting toolbars share a single row, so that you have more room for your work. You can disable this option from the **Options** tab, or you can toggle the option by clicking the drop-down arrow at the end of either the Standard or Formatting toolbar and selecting **Show Buttons on One Row or Show Buttons on Two Rows** as required.

Don't panic if your toolbars and menus are not exactly the same as those in this book.

1.7 Menus

There are nine main menus in your PowerPoint application window. You can use these menus to access any function or feature available in PowerPoint. I suggest you have a browse through them to get an idea of what's available – some menu items on the lists may appear familiar to you, some will be new.

You can display a menu and select menu options using either the mouse or the keyboard.

Using the mouse

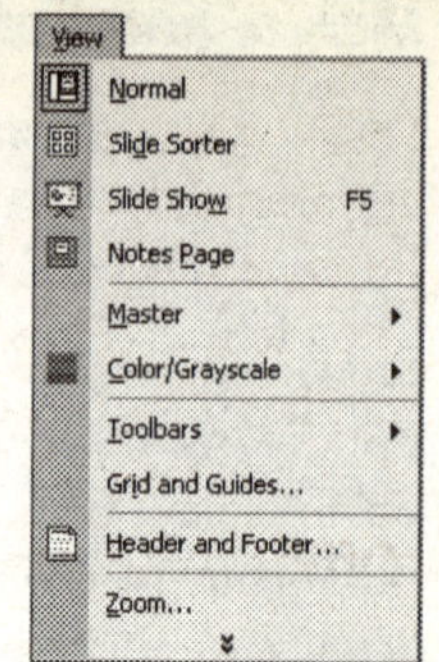

1 Click on the menu name to display the list of options available in that menu
2 Click on the menu item you wish to use

- Click the extension arrow at the bottom of your personalized menu to display all the options available.

Using the Keyboard

Each menu name has one character underlined.

To open a menu:

- Hold down the [**Alt**] key and press the underlined letter e.g. [**Alt**]-[**F**] for the **File** menu, [**Alt**]-[**I**] for the **Insert** menu.

Each item in a menu list also has a letter underlined in it. To select an item from the menu list either:

- Press the appropriate letter, or
- Use the up and down arrow keys on your keyboard until the item you want is selected, then press [**Enter**].

Once a menu list is displayed, you can press the right or left arrow keys to move from one menu to another.

To close a menu without selecting an item from the list:

- Click the menu name again, click anywhere off the menu list or press the [**Esc**] key on your keyboard.

In addition to the menus, many of the commands can be initiated using the toolbars, keyboard shortcuts or shortcut menus. Each of these areas will be covered as you progress through the book.

1.8 Help!

As you work with PowerPoint you will most probably find that you come a bit unstuck from time to time and need help! There are several ways to get help – most very intuitive and user friendly.

Ask a question box

You can access the Help system using the **Ask a question box** on the Menu bar. Simply type in your question and press **[Enter]**. Choose the Help topic required from the list that is displayed – click on it.

how do I insert a picture
- Add a picture
- Troubleshoot pictures
- Troubleshoot scanners and digital cameras
- Add data to a chart
- Troubleshoot toolbars and menus
- See more...

Office Assistant

To call on the Office Assistant, press **[F1]**, click the PowerPoint Help tool or click the Assistant icon on the Task Bar .

Depending on what you have been doing, the Assistant may display a list of topics that you might be interested in.

If you have a specific question you want to ask, type it in at the prompt and click the **Search** button.

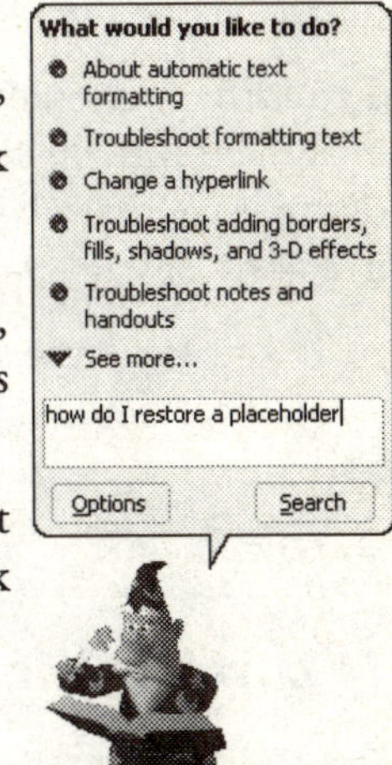

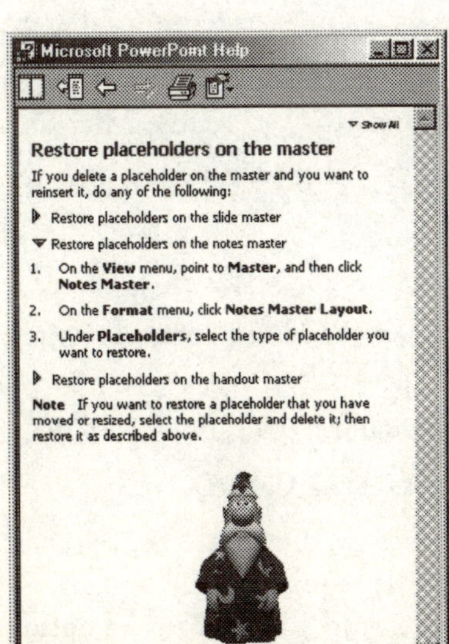

To choose a topic from the **What would you like to do?** list, simply click on the topic.

The Assistant will display the Help page.

The blue text on a Help page is a 'hot spot' that will display some information. The most common types of hot spots are:

- Bulleted item – displays a list of instructions when clicked.

- Embedded item – a word or phrase that has an explanation or definition attached to it. Simply click the coloured text to display the definition (usually displayed in green text).
- Tip – click it to see what it is.
- Show All – click to expand/collapse all the hot spots on the page.

When you've finished exploring the Help system, click the **Close** button at the top right of the Help window.

The Office Assistant can remain visible as you work on your document, or you can hide it and call on it as required. If you opt to leave it displayed, drag it to an area of your screen where it doesn't obscure your work.

- If you leave the Office Assistant displayed, left-click on it any time you want to ask a question.
- To hide the Office Assistant, right-click on it and choose **Hide** from the pop-up menu.

To customize the Office Assistant

You can customize the Office Assistant to take on a different appearance, or behave in a different way.

1 Show the Office Assistant (press [**F1**], click the Microsoft PowerPoint Help tool or on the Task Bar)

2 Click the **Options** button

3 To change its appearance, select the **Gallery** tab and browse through the options (use the **Next** and **Back** buttons to move through the various guises)

- If you find an Assistant you would like to use, click **OK**.
- To leave the Assistant as it was, click **Cancel**.

4 To change its behaviour, select the **Options** tab, select or deselect the options available as required – click on an option to switch it on or off. A tick in a box means an option is selected, an empty box means it isn't.

- If you don't want to use the Assistant, you can switch it off on the **Options** tab – simply deselect the **Use the Office Assistant** checkbox.

5 Click **OK** to set the options selected or **Cancel** to leave things as they were.

> **Tips**
>
> The Office Assistant is constantly monitoring your actions. If it thinks that it has a tip that may be useful to you, a light bulb will light up beside it. To read its tip, click the bulb.
>
> 

What's This?

If you haven't used Microsoft Office products before, or if you're new to the Windows environment, there may be many tools, menus, buttons and areas on your screen that puzzle you. The *What's This?* feature can help you here – it works best when a file is open, as most of the tools, menus and screen areas are then active.

To find out what a tool does:

1 Hold down the **[Shift]** key and press **[F1]**

2 Click the tool

To find out about an item in a menu list:

1 Hold down the **[Shift]** key and press **[F1]**

2 Open the menu list and select the option required from the list

To find out about anything else within the application window:

1 Hold down the **[Shift]** key and press **[F1]**

2 Click on the item

If you accidentally invoke the *What's This* help option, press **[Shift]**-**[F1]** (or the **[Esc]** key) to cancel it.

- Whether or not you use the Office Assistant, the Microsoft PowerPoint Help tool will open the on-line Help system. You can also access the system from the Help menu .

Help tabs

There are a number of Help tabs that can be displayed, called **Contents, Answer Wizard** or **Index**, and you can interrogate the Help system using them.

Click the tool to toggle the display of the tabs.

Contents tab

You can browse through the Help system from the Contents tab.

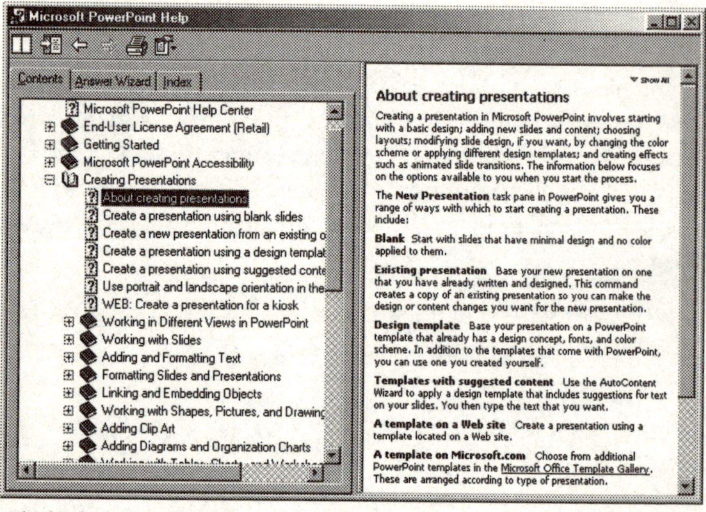

Click the + to the left of a book to display or to hide its list of contents.

When a book is open, you will be presented with a list of topics

To display a topic:

1 Click on it

2 Work through the Help system until you find the help you need

To print a topic:

- Click the **Print** tool in the Help dialog box when the topic is displayed.

To revisit pages you've already been to:

- Click the **Back** tool or **Forward** tool to go back and forward through the pages.

Close the Help window when you're finished.

Answer Wizard

You can interrogate the Help system on the Answer Wizard tab.

1 Enter your question, e.g. *How do I print out handouts* and click **Search**

2 Select a topic from the *Select topic to display* list. The Help page will be displayed

- If you can't find what you're looking for you could try the Web – click the **Search on Web** button at the bottom of the **Answer Wizard** tab.

Index tab

If you know what you are looking for, the Index tab gives you quick access to any topic and is particularly useful once you are familiar with the terminology used in PowerPoint.

1 At the **Microsoft PowerPoint Help** dialog box, select the **Index** tab

2 Type the word you're looking for in the *Type Keywords* field and click **Search**

Or

- Double-click on a word in the *Or choose keywords* list

3 Choose a topic from the *Choose a topic* list

4 Work through the Help system until you find what you need

5 Close the Help window when you've finished

ScreenTips

If you point to any tool on a toolbar, a ScreenTip will probably appear to describe the purpose of the tool. If no ScreenTips appear, you can easily switch them on if you want to.

If you like using keyboard shortcuts, you may find it useful to customize the basic ScreenTip, so that it displays the keyboard shortcut for a command as well. This might help you learn the keyboard shortcuts more quickly.

To customize ScreenTips:

1 Point to any toolbar and click the right mouse button
2 Choose **Customize…** from the shortcut menu
3 In the **Customize** dialog box select the **Options** tab
4 To switch the ScreenTips on, select the **Show ScreenTips on toolbars** option (or deselect this to switch them off)
5 Select the **Show shortcut keys in ScreenTips** option to have the keyboard shortcut for each tool displayed in the ScreenTip
6 Click **Close**

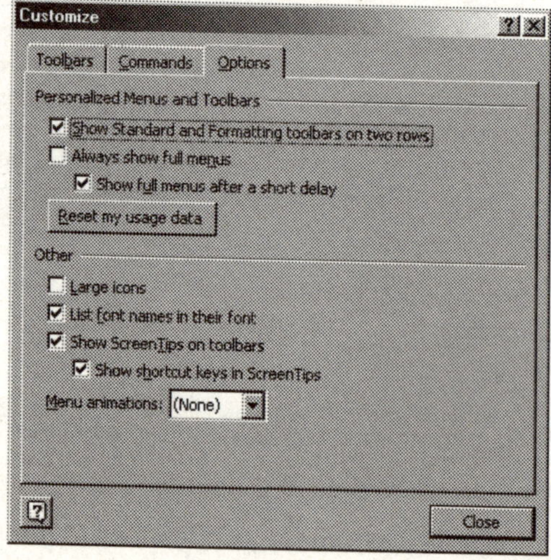

Dialog Box Help

When you access a dialog box in PowerPoint, for example, the **Customize** one, you can get help on any item within it that you don't understand.

To get help on an item in a dialog box:

1 Click the **Help** button **?** at the right of the dialog box title bar

2 Click on the option, button or item in the dialog box that you want explained

- A brief explanation of the selected item will be displayed.

3 Click anywhere within the dialog box to cancel the explanation.

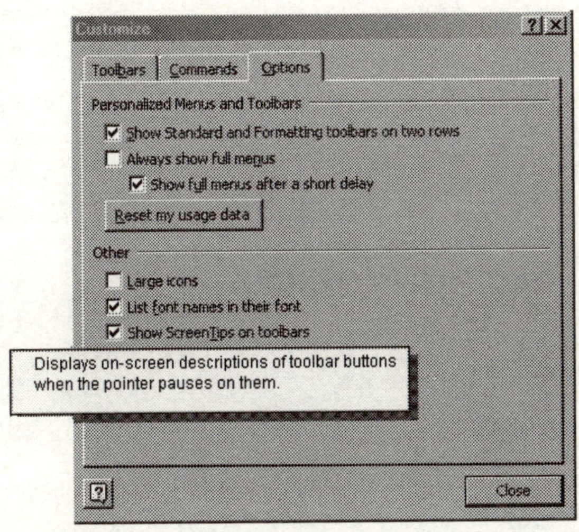

1.9 Help on the Internet

If you can't find the help you are looking for in the normal Help system, visit the Microsoft Office Assistance Centre to get updated Help files, answers to frequently asked questions on PowerPoint, tips, templates and answers to top support issues.

1 Open the **Help** menu
2 Choose **Office on the Web**
3 Navigate your way through the Help pages until you find the information required

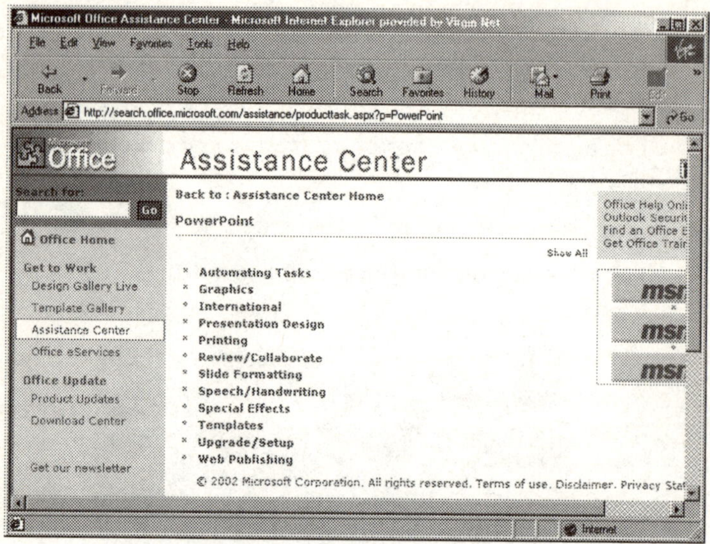

1.10 Exiting PowerPoint

When you have finished working in PowerPoint you must close the application down – don't just switch off your computer!

To exit PowerPoint

- Open the **File** menu and choose **Exit**

Or

- Click the **Close** button in the right-hand corner of the Application Title Bar.

If you have been working on a presentation but have not saved it you will be prompted to do so – see section 2.2.

Summary

In this chapter we have discussed:

- PowerPoint as a powerful presentation graphics package
- The minimum software and hardware requirements necessary to run the package successfully
- The installation procedure for the software
- PowerPoint objects
- Accessing the package through the Shortcut Bar and the Start menu
- The PowerPoint screen
- Utilizing the menu system using the mouse and the keyboard
- The Office Assistant and the On-line Help system
- Help from the Microsoft Office Assistance Center
- Exiting PowerPoint

02 basic powerpoint skills

In this chapter you will learn

- how to create, save, print, open and close presentations
- about the view options
- about the outline and slides pane, and the notes pane
- how to hide and restore panes
- how to move through slides

Aims of this chapter

In this chapter we will discuss the options for creating a new presentation and saving, closing and opening existing presentations. We will also discuss the different view options that are available when working on a presentation.

2.1 New presentations

When you start PowerPoint, a new Blank Presentation is created automatically, with a blank Title slide. The New Presentation Task Pane is displayed down the right of the screen (if the **Show at startup** checkbox at the bottom of the Task Pane has been deselected, the Task Pane will not appear at startup).

The boxes with dotted outlines that appear when you create a new slide are called *placeholders*. Different slide layouts have different placeholders set up on them. They will contain the title, text and any other objects you display on your slide.

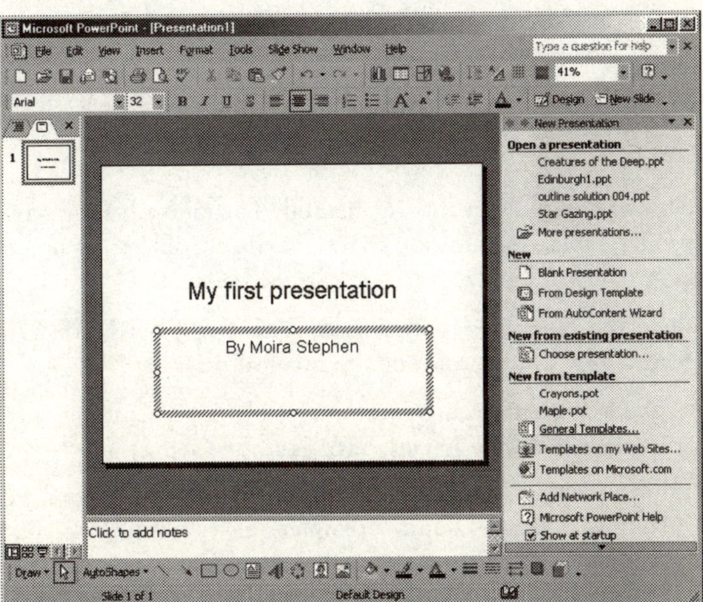

1 Follow the prompts on the slide – enter the title and sub-title (if required) for your presentation

2 Click the **New Slide** tool [New Slide] on the Formatting toolbar

3 Select a slide layout from the **Slide Layout** Task Pane (a single bulleted list layout is the default)

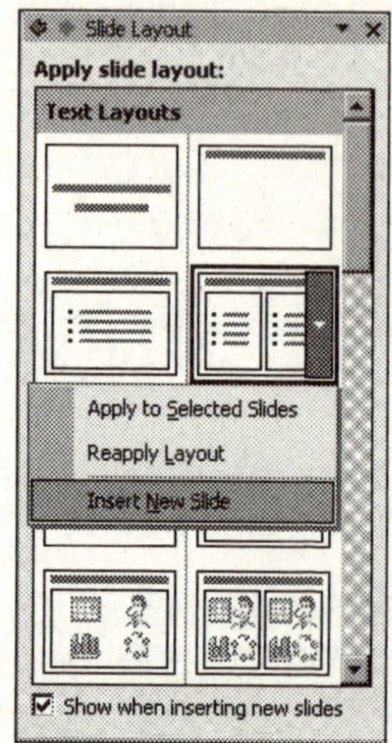

4 Enter your text – follow the prompts

5 Repeat steps 2 to 4 until all slides have been added

- We'll discuss the various objects later in the book.
- You can insert a slide from the **Slide Layout** Task Pane by clicking the drop-down arrow to the right of the slide icon, and clicking **Insert New Slide.**
- You can resize the Task Pane by clicking and dragging its left border.
- Use the arrows at the top left of the Task Pane to move between the **New Presentation** Task Pane and **Slide Layout** Task Pane.

Some of the slide layouts in the Slide Layout Task Pane have graphic, table, organization chart and clip art objects set up on them. We will look at these later in the book.

When the New Presentation Task Pane is displayed, you can create a new presentation in a number of ways.

- **Blank Presentation** creates a new blank presentation and displays the **Slide Layout** Task Pane (see above).
- **From Design Template** first displays the **Slide Design** Task Pane so you can choose a template on which to base your presentation (this will determine the design of the presentation, including font and colour scheme)

- **From AutoContent Wizard** creates a new presentation and starts a wizard to step you through the process of setting up your title slide, outline of presentation and colour scheme

Design Template

To create a new presentation using the Design Template:

1 Click **From Design Template** on the **New Presentation** Task Pane

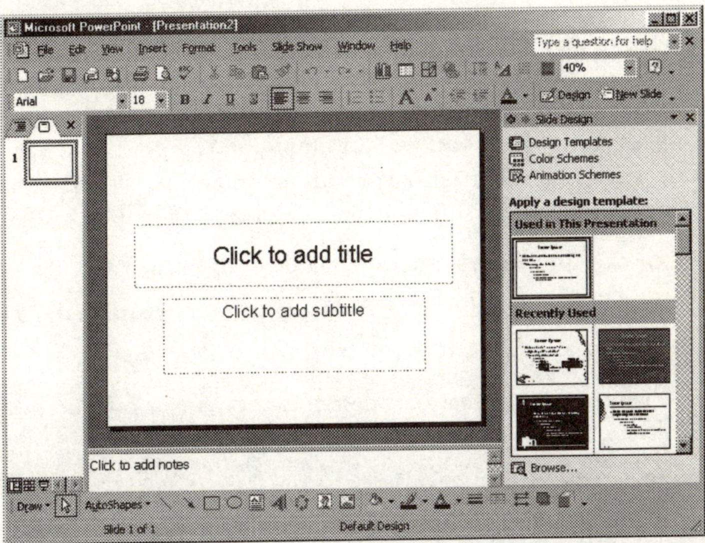

2 Select a template from those listed (or click **Browse...** and locate the template you wish to use)

3 Complete the Title Slide, replacing the prompts, e.g. *Click to add title*, with your own text

4 Click the New Slide tool on the Formatting toolbar

5 Select the layout for your next slide

6 Follow the instructions on the slide to complete it

7 Repeat steps 4 to 6 until all slides have been added

If you don't like the look of your selected template, change it from the **Slide Design** Task Pane.

To display the Slide Design Task Pane:

- Click the **Design** tool on the Formatting toolbar

Or

- Click the arrows at the top left of the Task Pane until the **Slide Design** Task Pane is displayed

Or

- Double-click on the template name on the Status Bar

AutoContent Wizard

This sets up several slides – the exact number depends on the choices you make as you work through the Wizard. If you need help setting up the structure of your presentation, or need some ideas on what to put on your slides, this option may be useful.

1 Click **From AutoContent Wizard** on the Task Pane
2 The first time you run the Wizard the Office Assistant dashes to your aid! Close it if you wish and click
3 Pick the option that best describes the type of presentation you are going to give.
4 Select the presentation style – on-screen, Web, overheads or slides.
5 Enter the presentation title and any information that you want displayed in the slide footer area
6 At the last screen click . PowerPoint will set up your presentation

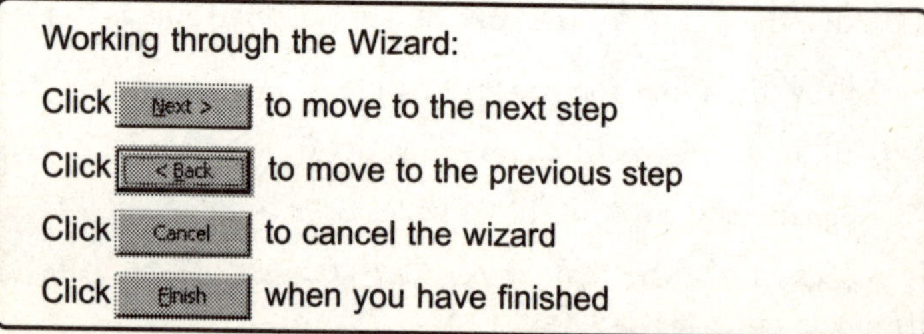

- Once a presentation has been created (using any of the above options), you can easily add or delete slides, change slide layouts or change the design template used as required.

You can create a new blank presentation by clicking the **New** tool on the Standard toolbar, or by pressing **[Ctrl]-[N]** on your keyboard.

- You can display the **New Presentation** Task Pane by opening the **File** menu and choosing **New…** or open the **View** menu and choose **Task Pane**.

2.2 Saving a presentation

Once you have set up your presentation, you must save it if you want to keep it (if you don't save it, it will be lost when you close PowerPoint or switch off your computer).

1. Click the **Save** tool on the Standard Toolbar
2. Specify the drive and/or folder into which you wish to save your presentation
3. Give your presentation a file name

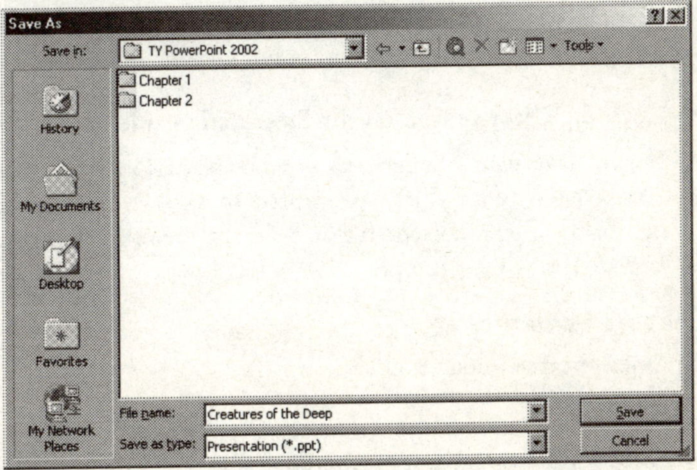

Save vs Save As

The first time you save a presentation, you are taken to the **Save As** dialog box where you specify the drive and/or folder that you want your file saved in, and give your presentation a name. Thereafter, any time you save the presentation using the **Save** tool on the toolbar, the old version of the file is replaced by the new, edited version. This is what you would usually want to happen.

However, if you have saved your presentation, gone on to edit it, then wish to save the edited version using a different filename, or in a different location, open the **File** menu and choose **Save As** to get to the **Save As** dialog box.

2.3 Closing and opening files

When you've finished working on your presentation you must save it (see above) and close it.

Leaving PowerPoint is very easy. If you use other Windows packages, the technique is very similar.

Closing a presentation

- Open the **File** menu and choose **Close**.

Or

- Click the **Close** button on the Presentation title bar.
- If you have made changes to your presentation since you last saved it, you will be prompted to save your changes before the file is closed. If you want to save the changes, choose **Yes** at the prompt.

Leaving PowerPoint

1 Open the **File** menu and choose **Exit**.

Or

- Click the **Close** button on the PowerPoint title bar.

Opening a presentation

If you want to work on a presentation you've already created, saved and closed, you must open it first.

1 Click the **Open** tool on the Standard toolbar.

Or

- Open the **File** menu and choose **Open**.

2 Select the drive and folder that contains your presentation file.

3 Double-click on the name or select the presentation name and click Open

- Recently used files are displayed on the **New Presentation** Task Pane and at the end of the **File** menu – to open one simply click on its name.

2.4 View options

When working on a presentation, there are three view options to choose from:

- Normal view
- Slide Sorter view
- Slide Show

By default, PowerPoint opens a presentation in **Normal** view.

Use the View icons at the bottom left of the screen to get a different view of your presentation. You can also change views using the **View** menu.

The **View** menu has an additional option called **Notes Page** view. This displays a miniature of your slide, with the notes area below it, which is how your notes will look when printed. You can enter and edit your notes in this view. If you wish to do this, use the **Zoom** tool on the Standard toolbar to zoom into about 75% so that you can read the text.

In **Slide Sorter** view each slide is displayed in miniature – this view can be used for moving slides around and to help you prepare for the actual presentation. We will discuss this view later in the book.

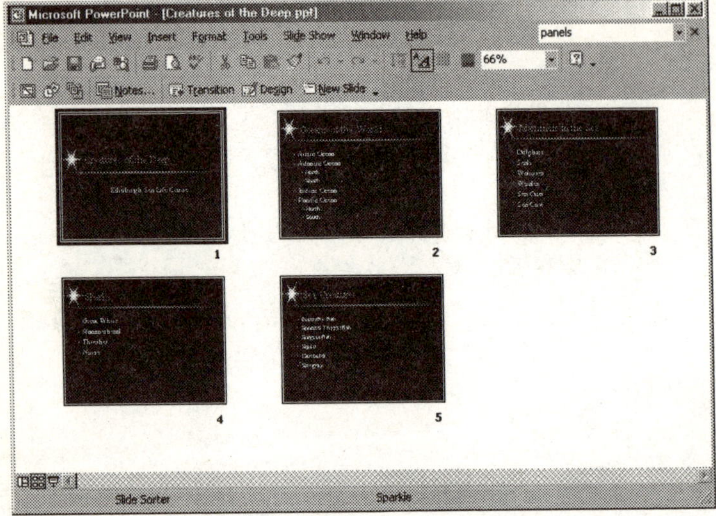

Slide Show view can be useful at any time to let you see how your slide will look in the final presentation. Press [**Esc**] from Slide Show view to return to your presentation file.

The view that you will use when setting up your presentation is **Normal** view. In Normal view, you have three panes displaying different parts of your presentation: the slide itself, a notes pane displayed at the bottom and the outline and slide tabs displayed down the left.

A Task Pane will often be displayed too.

2.5 Outline and Slides pane

In Normal view the Outline and Slides pane is displayed down the left of the screen.

The Outline tab displays the text on each slide, with a slide icon to the left of each slide title.

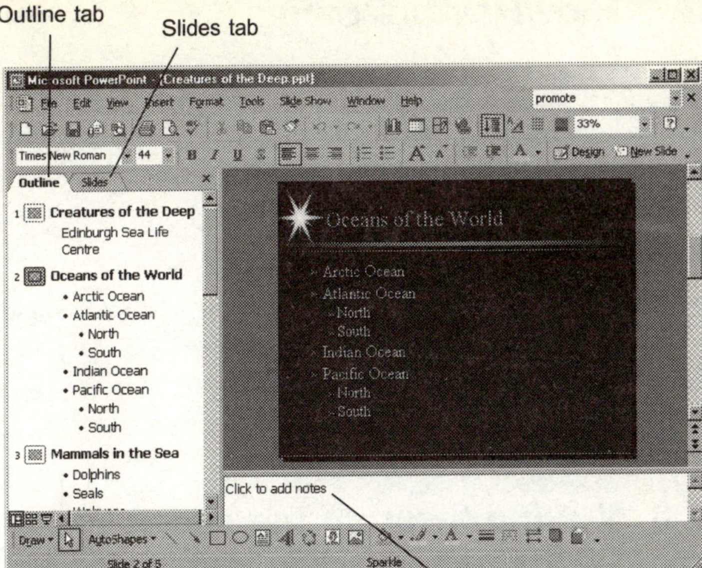

You can insert and delete text in the Outline tab just as you would on the Slide itself.

You can select a slide on the Outline tab by clicking the slide icon to the left of the title.

The Slides tab shows miniatures of the slides in the presentation.

2.6 Notes pane

As the presenter of a presentation, you may wish to add some notes (that you can use during your presentation) to some of your slides.

Notes are added to the Notes pane, below the Slide pane.

To add notes:

1 Click in the **Notes** pane

2 Type in your notes

We will discuss notes more fully in Chapter 9.

2.7 Hide/Restore panes

Hide

- Click the **Close** button at the top right of the Outline and Slides pane. Both the Outline and Slides pane and the Notes pane disappear.

Restore

- Click the **Normal** view icon or open the View menu and choose **Normal (Restore Panes)**.

You can resize the panes if you wish – click and drag the pane border to do so.

2.8 Moving through the slides

To move through the slides in your presentation:

- Click on the slide that you wish to display on the Slides tab

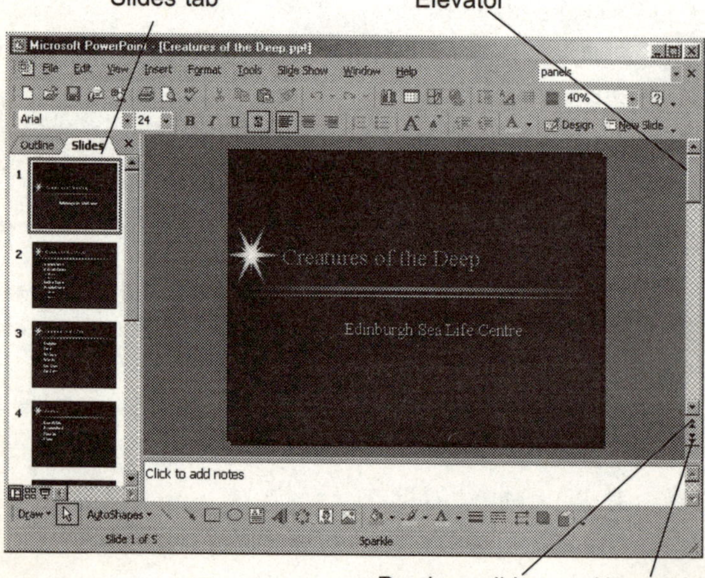

Or

- Click the **Next** or **Previous Slide** buttons at the bottom of the vertical scroll bar

Or

- Drag the elevator on the vertical scroll bar up and down (let go when you reach the required slide)

Summary

This chapter has introduced what you need to know to get started using PowerPoint.

We have discussed:

- Creating a new presentation using the Blank Presentation, Design Template and AutoContent Wizard
- Adding slides to a presentation
- Saving a presentation, including Save vs Save As
- Closing a presentation
- Opening a presentation
- The view options available in a presentation
- The Outline and Slides pane
- The Notes pane
- Hiding and Restoring the panes
- Resizing the panes
- Moving through your slides

In this chapter you will learn

- how to add, delete, move and copy slides
- how to format text
- about indents, numbering and bullet points
- how to change the slide layout and the template
- how to add comments to slides

Aims of this chapter

In this chapter we will discuss adding and removing slides and moving slides. We will also discuss structuring the bullet points on a slide, rearranging the order of the bullets and numbering the points on a slide (rather than using bullets).

3.1 Adding and deleting slides

We discussed adding slides to a presentation in the previous chapter. We added slides in Normal view in Chapter 2, but you can also add slides in Slide Sorter view. The method is the same in either view.

Adding a slide

If the **Slide Layout** Task Pane is not displayed:

1 View (or select in Slide Sorter view) the slide that will go *before* the slide you are going to add

2 Click the New Slide tool on the **Formatting** toolbar

3 Choose a slide layout from the **Slide Layout** Task Pane

If the Slide Layout Task Pane is open:

1 View (or select in Slide Sorter view) the slide that will go *before* the slide you are going to add

2 Click the drop-down arrow to the right of the slide layout that you wish to insert

3 Click **Insert New Slide**

Deleting a slide

In Normal view

1 View the slide that you wish to delete
2 Open the **Edit** menu and click **Delete Slide**

In the Outline and Slides pane or in Slide Sorter view:

1 Right-click on the slide that you wish to delete
2 Left-click on **Delete slide**

3.2 Moving or copying a slide

This can be done in the Outline and Slides pane or in Slide Sorter view.

Drag and drop

1 Select the slide that you wish to move
2 To move the slide – drag and drop it (watching the dimmed line to check your position)

Or

- To copy the slide – hold the [**Ctrl**] key down while you drag and drop it

Cut or copy and paste

1 Select the slide that you wish to move
2 Click the **Cut** tool (or the **Copy** tool) on the Standard toolbar
3 Select the slide that you want to precede the slide you are moving or copying
4 Click the **Paste** tool on the Standard toolbar

Cut or Copy

When you drag and drop or cut and paste a slide, the slide is actually *moved* from one place to another.

If you [Ctrl]-drag and drop or copy and paste a slide, the original slide remains where it is, and a copy is created where you drop or paste the slide.

3.3 Formatting text

So far, we've accepted the font formats set by PowerPoint. You can change these at any time using the Formatting toolbar.

To change the font name, size, style or colour:

1 Select the text you want to format

2 Drop down the **Font** list and choose one

Or

- Drop down the colour palette by clicking the drop-down arrow to the right of the **Font Color** tool, and choose one

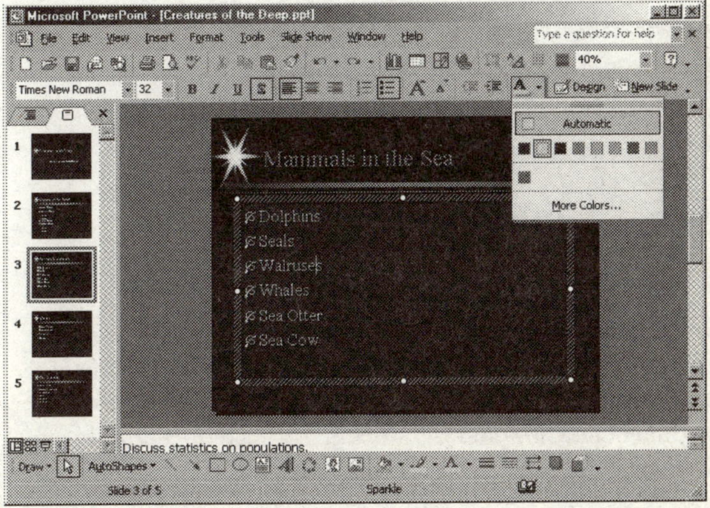

Or

- Drop down the **Font size** list and choose one

Or

- Click the **Bold, Italic, Underline** or **Shadow** tools to switch the format on and off.

3 Deselect the text.

> **Useful keyboard shortcuts**
>
> [Ctrl]-[B] Bold [Ctrl]-[I] Italics
> [Ctrl]-[U] Underline
>
> These all toggle the effect on and off

- You can change the size of selected text by clicking [A] to increase or [A] to decrease it to the next size in the Font Size list.

You can also go to the **Font** dialog box to format the text on your slides.

1 Select the text to be formatted
2 Choose **Font…** from the **Format** menu
3 Set the formatting options as required
4 Click **OK**

3.4 Paragraph formatting

Alignment

In presentations, text is usually aligned to the left or centre. There are tools for both of these and for right alignment on the Formatting toolbar. If you want text justified (making the text meet both left and right margins), open the **Format** menu, point to **Alignment** and select **Justify**.

1 Select the text you want to format

2 Click the **Left**, **Center** or **Right** 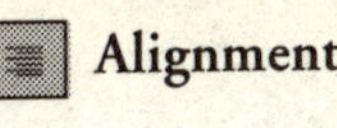 **Alignment** tool

3 If you have selected multiple paragraphs or several characters, deselect the text

> **Useful keyboard shortcuts**
>
> [Ctrl]-[L] Left Align   [Ctrl]-[R] Right Align
> [Ctrl]-[E] Centre   [Ctrl]-[J] Justify

- A paragraph is selected if the insertion point is within it, or at least part of it is highlighted – you don't need to select all the characters.

Levels of indent (promoting and demoting points)

The text on your slide can be structured into main points and sub-points if necessary (using up to 5 levels).

> Slide Title
>
> Level 1
>   Level 2
>   Level 3
>   Level 4
>   Level 5

The default level for a bullet point is Level 1.

You can easily increase the indent of bullet points so that you create sub-points under your main points if required. You can decrease the indent again if you change your mind.

To increase or decrease the indent on a bullet point:

Using the toolbar

1 Click anywhere within the bullet point you wish to demote (either on your slide or on the Outline tab)

Oceans of the World

- Arctic Ocean
- Atlantic Ocean
  - North
  - South
- Indian Ocean
- Pacific Ocean
  - North
  - South

2 Click the **Increase Indent** tool on the Formatting toolbar to demote the bullet, or the **Decrease Indent** tool to promote the bullet

Drag

You can also drag the bullet points to the level required.

1 Move the mouse pointer over the bullet (it becomes a four-headed arrow when the mouse is in the correct position)

2 Drag the bullet right or left to the required level (the mouse pointer will become a two-headed arrow as you drag)

Using the keyboard

1 Place the insertion point before the text that you wish to increase or decrease the indent of

2 Press [**Tab**] to increase the indent

Or

- Press [**Shift**]-[**Tab**] to decrease the indent

3.5 Rearranging the bullet points

If you have entered your text, and then decide that it is not in the correct order, you can move the bullet points within (or between) slides.

To move the points within a slide:

Cut or copy and paste

1 Select the bullet point that you wish to move

2 Click the **Cut** tool (or the **Copy** tool) on the Standard toolbar

3 Place the insertion point at the beginning of the text in the bullet point that will go below the point that you are moving or copying

4 Click the **Paste** tool on the Standard toolbar

Drag

You can also drag the bullet points to the position required.

1 Move the mouse pointer over the bullet (it becomes a four-headed arrow when the mouse is in the correct position)

2 Drag the bullet up or down to the required position (the pointer will become a two-headed arrow as you drag)

Using the keyboard

1 Place the insertion point within the text that you wish to move up or down

2 Press **[Alt]-[Shift]-[Up arrow]** to move the point up

Or

- Press **[Alt]-[Shift]-[Down arrow]** to move the point down

Numbering the points

There may be times that you would rather number your points than use bullets. You can use the **Numbering** tool on the Formatting toolbar for this.

1 Select the points that you want numbered

2 Click the **Numbering** tool 

Numbered points can be promoted, demoted and moved in the same way as bulleted points.

Removing bullets or numbers

You will nearly always want the points on your slide to be bulleted or numbered for easy identification. There may, however, be odd occasions when you wish to switch the bullets or numbers off altogether.

To switch the bullets or numbers off:

1 Select the points on your slide
2 If the points are bulleted, click the **Bullets** tool to switch them off

Or

- If the points are numbered, click the **Numbering** tool to switch them off.

Customized bullets

The bullet style will normally be picked up from the Design Template used for the presentation. As an alternative, you could select a bullet from the **Bullets and Numbering** dialog box.

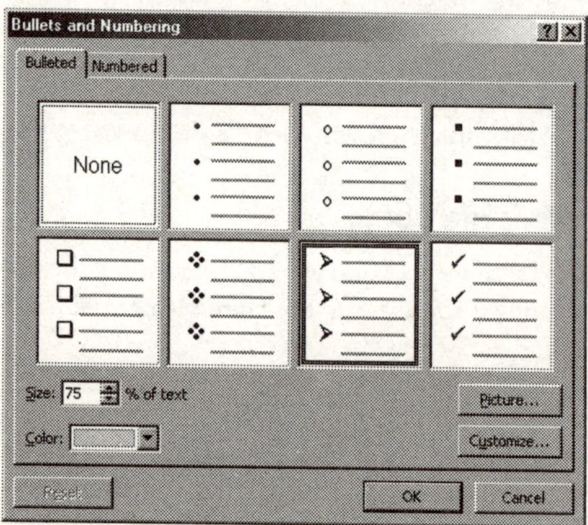

1 Select the point(s)
2 Open the **Format** menu and choose **Bullets and Numbering**
3 Click on the **Bulleted** tab
4 Select a bullet
5 Set the size and colour as required
6 Click **OK**

You could also choose a different character from one of the fonts available for your bullet point.

1 Work through steps 1 to 3 above
2 Click **Customize…**
3 In the **Symbol** dialog box, select a font from the list and choose a character – click on it

Or

- Select a character from the **Recently used symbols:** row

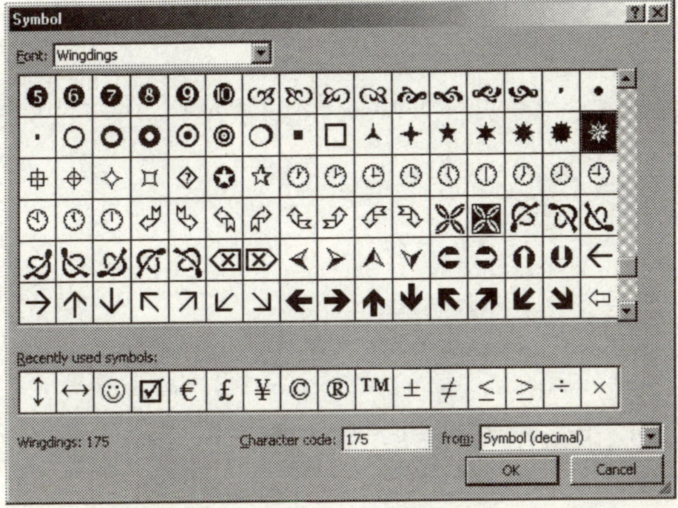

4 Click **OK** to close the **Symbol** dialog box
5 Click **OK** to close the **Bullets and Numbering** dialog box

- Alternatively, you can choose a picture bullet if you click **Picture...** in the **Bullets and Numbering** dialog box, and select a bullet from those available.
- You can customize the numbering style used from the **Numbered** tab in the **Bullets and Numbering** dialog box.

3.6 Changing a slide layout

1 In Normal view, display the slide whose layout you wish to change or select the slide in Slide Sorter view

2 Click the Layout tool or open the **Format** menu and choose **Slide Layout...** to display the Task Pane

3 Click the layout you want to use

3.7 Changing the design template

When you create a presentation using the Blank Presentation option, the default design template is used. You can change the design template at any time.

- Click Design on the **Formatting** toolbar to display the **Slide Design** Task Pane

To apply the layout to all slides:

- Click on the design template that you want to use, or click the drop down arrow to the right of the layout and choose **Apply to All Slides**

To apply to the selected slide – the one you are looking at in Normal view, or the one(s) selected in Slide Sorter view:

- Click the drop-down arrow to the right of the layout required and choose **Apply to Selected Slides**

You may have a presentation with more than one design template, e.g. a different template for different sections of your presentation.

3.8 Comments

If you are working on a presentation and wish to add a comment to a slide, perhaps a reminder to yourself to check something, you can use Comments. The comments will not be displayed when you give your presentation. You have the option of printing any comments out when you print your presentation (see Chapter 11).

To add a comment to a slide:

1 Display the slide in Normal view

2 Open the **Insert** menu

3 Choose **Comment**

4 Type in your comment

5 Press **[Esc]** or click anywhere on your slide when you have finished

A comment marker is displayed on the slide in Normal view. If you place your mouse pointer over the marker, the comment will be displayed.

To edit a comment:

1 Right-click on it

2 Left click on **Edit Comment**

3 Update the comment as necessary

4 Press **[Esc]** or click anywhere on your slide when you have finished.

To delete a comment:

1 Right-click on it

2 Left click on **Delete Comment**

Summary

This chapter has discussed:

- Adding slides
- Deleting slides
- Moving and copying slides
- Formatting text
- Increasing and decreasing the indent on bullet points
- Moving bullet points
- Numbering points
- Removing bullets and numbers from points
- Customizing bullet points
- Changing the slide layout
- Applying a design template
- Adding, editing and deleting comments

drawing

In this chapter you will learn

- about drawing objects
- how to add special effects to drawing objects
- what AutoShapes are
- how to change the order, and group and ungroup objects
- how to create WordArt objects

Aims of this chapter

So far, we have dealt with text objects – slide headings and points listed for discussion on the slides. In this chapter we will consider some of the other objects that you may want to place on your slide. Moving, resizing and deleting objects, drawings tools, AutoShapes, rotating and grouping objects, and WordArt will be discussed.

4.1 The Drawing toolbar

The Drawing toolbar is normally displayed along the bottom of the window.

Select objects

The **Select Objects** tool is selected unless you select another tool from the toolbar. It is used to select any object on your slide – not just drawings. Once an object has been selected, you can move it, resize it, delete it (and lots of other things as we'll soon see). Work in Normal view for this section.

To select a text object:

1 Position the mouse pointer over any text within the placeholder area and click

- Note the handles that appear at the corners and along the edges of the selected object.

To select other objects:

2 Click anywhere inside the object placeholder

To deselect an object:

3 Click anywhere outside the selected object

To move an object:

- Point to the border of a text object, or anywhere within any

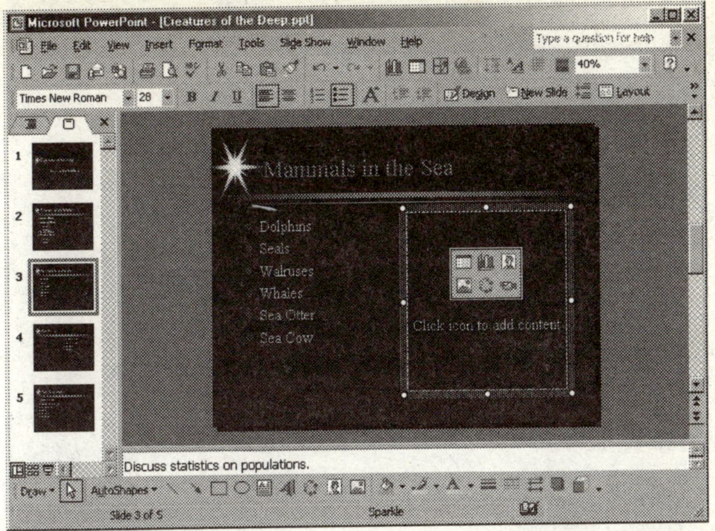

other type of object (not a handle) and drag the object to its new position.

To resize an object:

- Point to one of the handles (note the mouse pointer) and drag the handle until the object is the required size

To delete a text object:

- Select the text object, click the border once, then press **[Delete]**.

To delete other objects:

- Select, and then press **[Delete]**.
- If you delete an object by mistake, click the **Undo** tool on the Standard toolbar.

4.2 Text box tool

You can use the Text box tool to enter text anywhere on your slide (not necessarily within an existing text placeholder).

1 Select the **Text Box** tool
2 Click anywhere on your slide to position the insertion point

3 Key in the text

4 Format the text as required

The text object you have created can be selected, moved, resized and deleted.

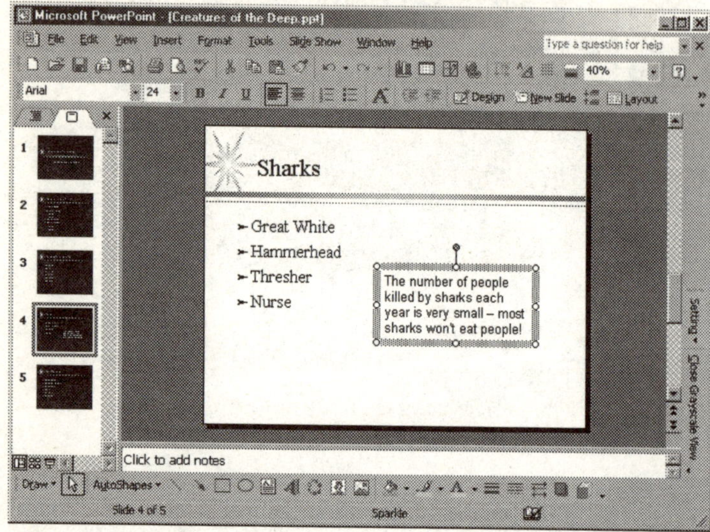

You can format the text using any of the formatting options – bold, size, font style, italics, underline, etc.

Text objects can be placed in an AutoShape to add emphasis, or rotated to create interesting effects on your slides (see 4.4).

4.3 Drawing tools

The line, arrow, rectangle and oval tools all work in a similar way. You can customize a shape in many ways – give it a shadow or 3-D effect, change the line colour and thickness, or experiment with fill colours and patterns.

Experiment with the options on your slides.

To use the line-based tools:

1 Select a tool – line, arrow, rectangle or oval 

2 Click to set the start

3 Drag to draw the shape

- Hold [Shift] down as you click and drag if you want a straight line (line tool), a square (rectangle tool) or circle (oval tool).

Different effects

You can format the drawing objects by changing the fill colour or line colour, changing the line or arrow style, or giving the object a shadow or 3-D effect.

To format the object:

1 Select the object

- Change the Fill or Line colour
- Set the line, dash or arrow style
- Add a shadow or 3-D effect

2 Deselect the object

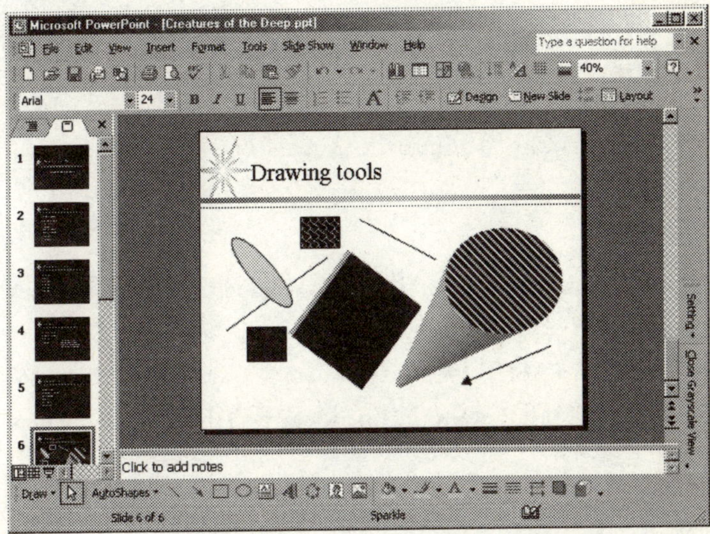

- If you need to draw several lines, arrows, rectangles or ovals, you can 'lock' the tool on by double-clicking on it. Draw as many shapes as you need, then select any other tool (or press [Esc]) to unlock it.

- To select a drawing object, click anywhere within it.

4.4 AutoShapes

You may find the shape you need under AutoShapes. If you want stars, triangles, arrows, etc. on your slide you'll find lots to choose from. AutoShapes can be drawn and formatted in the same way as the basic drawing shapes.

- The Freeform and Curve AutoShapes in the Line category don't quite follow the basic click and drag principle adopted by the other drawing tools.

Experiment with the options:

1 Click the AutoShapes tool to display the categories available

2 Select a category

3 Choose a shape

4 Click and drag on your slide to draw your shape

5 Drag a handle to adjust the shape

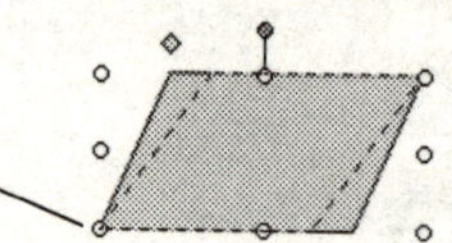

Freeform

6 Click and drag (note the pencil shaped pointer) to draw lines freehand

Or, to get a straight line

7 Click where you want the line to start, then click again where it will end

Curve

8 Click a path that you want the curve to follow

9 Double-click or press [Esc] when done to switch the tool off

- You can change the fill colour or pattern or line characteristics of any shape using the tools on the Drawing toolbar.

If you have used earlier versions of PowerPoint, you will find that there are even more AutoShapes to choose from in PowerPoint 2002.

1 Select **More AutoShapes...** from the AutoShapes list
2 Scroll through the list of AutoShapes displayed
3 Click on the shape that you want to insert

- Move and/or resize the shape as required.

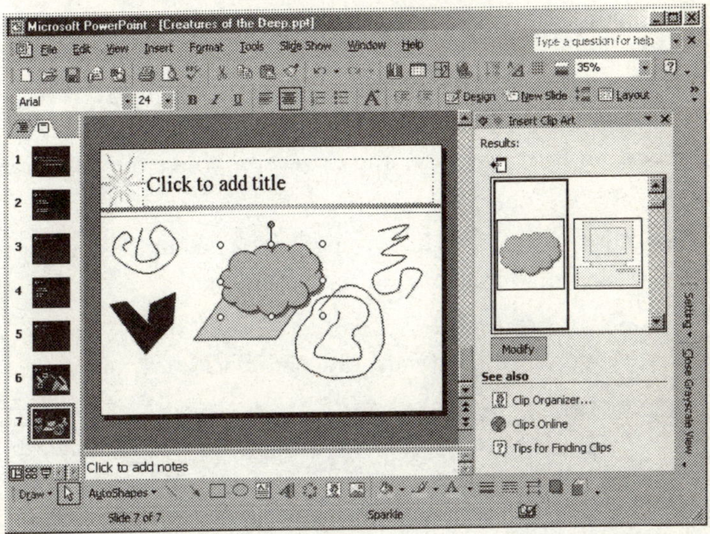

4.5 Rotate and Flip

Once an object has been drawn, you can flip it over horizontally or vertically, or rotate it right or left to get the effect you want.

1 Select the object you wish rotate
2 Drag the rotate handle to rotate the object

Or

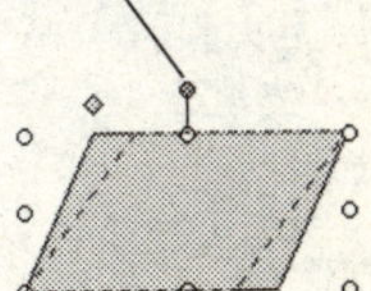

3 Choose **Rotate** or **Flip** from the **Draw** menu

4 Select the option required from the submenu – the **Rotate** options turn the object 90° right or left, the **Flip** options turn the object 180°.

- With the **Free Rotate** option, rotate handles appear on each corner of the object. Drag a rotate handle to turn the shape.
- The **Rotate** or **Flip** submenu can be dragged to float on your screen. Click and drag its title bar. Any submenu with a title bar can become a floating menu.

4.6 Changing the order

When you draw objects onto your slides, they lie in layers relative to the order in which they are drawn. The first object is on the bottom layer, the next one on a layer above the first one and so on.

Using this layering principle, you can create complex drawings by overlapping objects one on top of another.

If you need to rearrange the layering of your objects, you can do so using the **Bring Forward** and **Send Backward** commands.

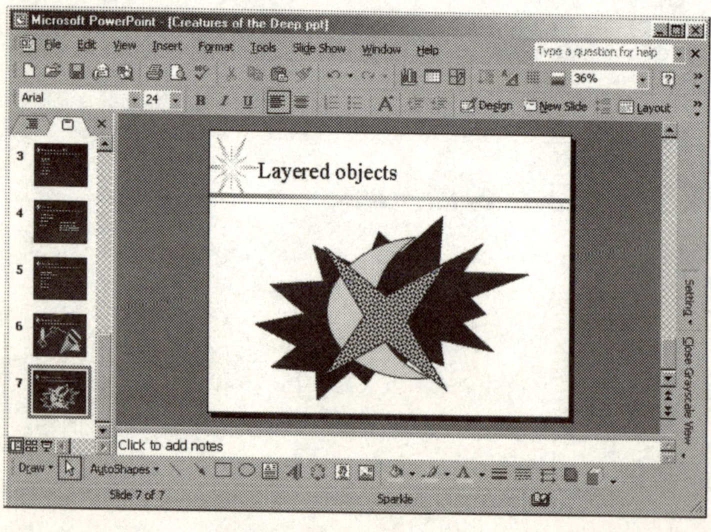

1 Select the object to **Bring Forward** or **Send Backward**

2 Open the **Draw** menu

3 Select **Order**

4 Choose the option required

- **Bring to Front** and **Send to Back** move the selected object to the top or bottom of the pile of objects. **Bring Forward** and **Send Backward** move the selected object through the pile one layer at a time.
- Right-click on the selected object to open the shortcut menu. Select **Order** from it and specify the options required.

4.7 Group and UnGroup

If you have drawn several objects to generate an image, you can group the objects together into one to make it easier to move, copy or resize the whole image.

1 Select the objects you want to group

- Select the first object then hold **[Shift]** down while you select the other objects.
- To select all the objects, use **[Ctrl]-[A]** or drag over them

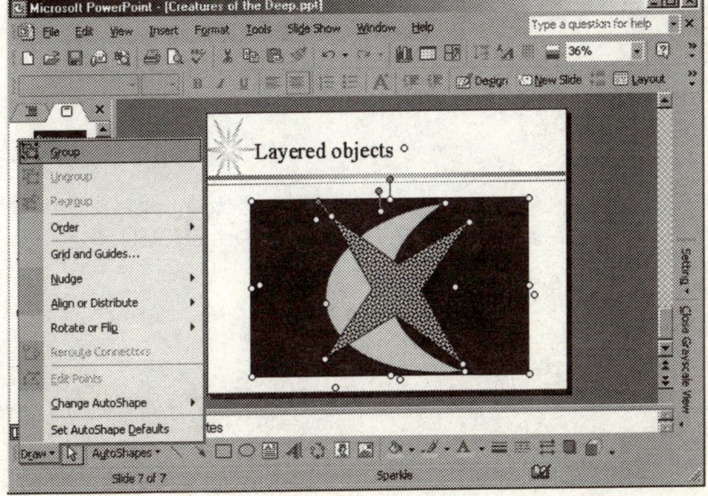

2 Open the **Draw** menu

3 Select **Group**

- To edit a grouped object, select it then use **Draw > Ungroup** to separate it into its original objects.

4.8 WordArt

WordArt lets you create special text effects. You can produce stunning title slides and real eye-catchers wherever they are needed.

1 Click the **Insert WordArt** tool

2 Select a WordArt style from the Gallery

3 Click **OK**

4 At the **Edit WordArt Text** dialog box, enter (and format) the text

5 Click **OK**

6 Adjust the shape of your WordArt object as required

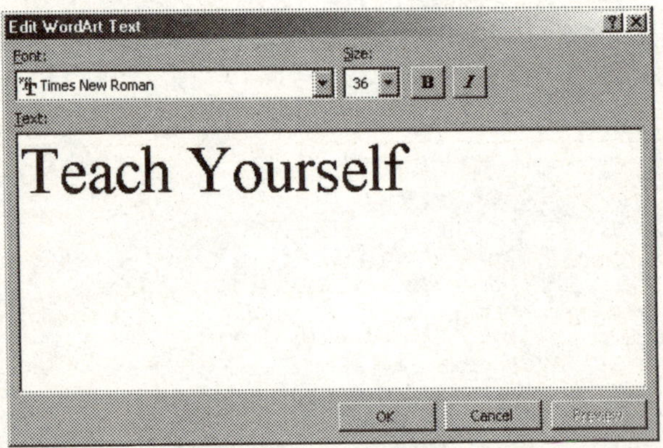

The WordArt toolbar

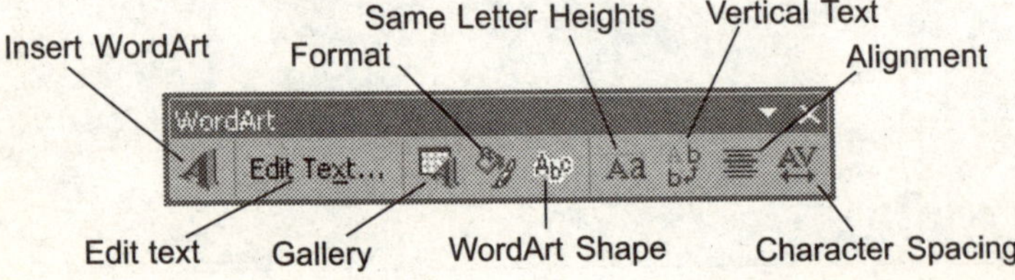

The shape drop-down menu

- Experiment with the tools to see the effects they produce.

Summary

This chapter has introduced:

- Moving, resizing and deleting objects
- The drawing tools
- Formatting drawing objects
- AutoShapes
- Rotating and grouping objects
- WordArt

05 charts

In this chapter you will learn

- how to create charts
- some chart formatting options
- how to import a chart from Excel

Aims of this chapter

Sometimes pictures can talk louder than words – and when this is the case you can use graphs, organization charts, clip art, tables, etc. to help you make your point. In this chapter we'll look at ways you can add a chart or graph to a slide. We will create charts, work with datasheets, change the chart type, and customize the chart in a variety of ways.

5.1 Creating a chart

You can create charts from scratch within PowerPoint or import them from Microsoft Excel. The default charting program used by PowerPoint is Microsoft Graph, which is installed automatically with PowerPoint.

There are three main ways to set up your chart.

- Choose a slide with a Chart placeholder from the **Slide Layout** Task Pane

Or

- Choose a new layout with a Content placeholder

Or

- Click the **Insert Chart** tool

Using a Chart placeholder

- Double-click within the Chart placeholder to add a chart

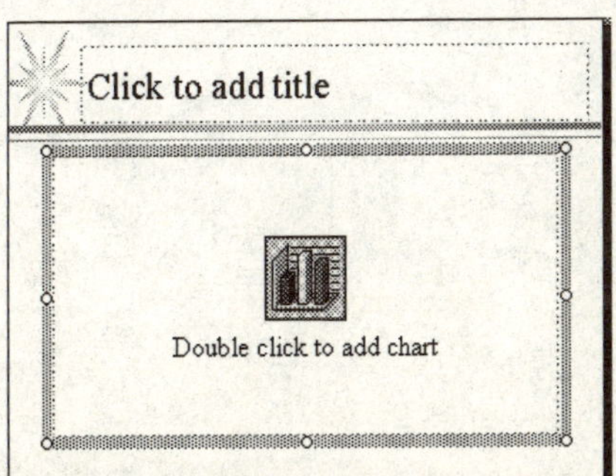

Using a Content placeholder

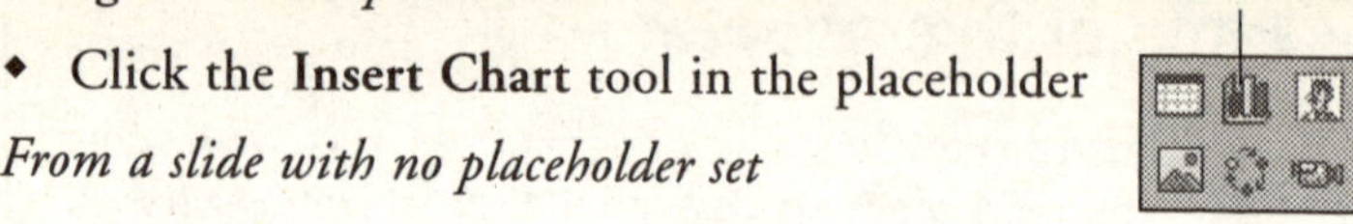

- Click the **Insert Chart** tool in the placeholder

From a slide with no placeholder set

- Click the **Insert Chart** tool on the Standard toolbar

5.2 Microsoft Graph

Regardless of how you decide to create your chart, Microsoft Graph opens and a chart window is displayed. This has its own Standard and Formatting toolbars, and you will notice a **Chart** menu appear on the Menu bar. The options in the other menus change to those suitable for working on charts.

There is also a small Datasheet window (which can be moved or resized as necessary), where you can key in the data that you want to chart. When working in Microsoft Graph the **Help** menu will give you access to help pages on the program.

- Explore the menus to see how they have changed.

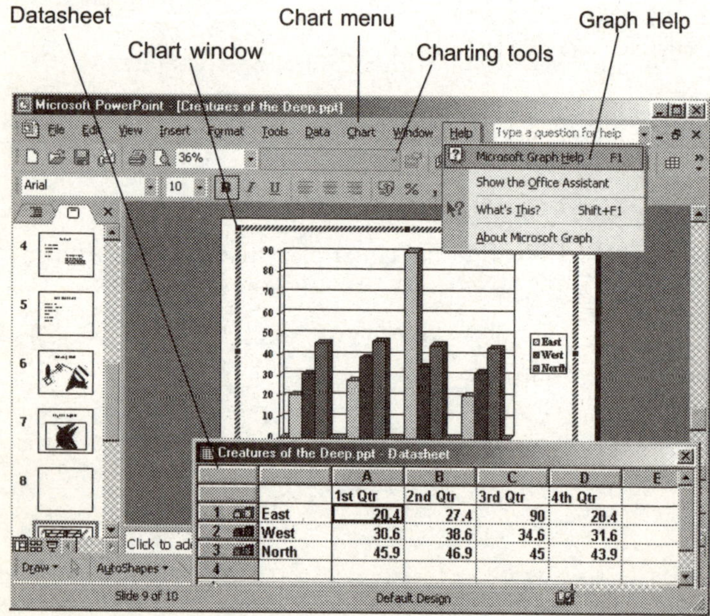

Entering your own data

You must replace the sample data in the datasheet with the data you want to chart. If you do not need to replace all the sample data, delete the cell contents that are not required – select the cell and press the **[Delete]** key on your keyboard.

1 Select the cell into which you wish to enter your own data
2 Key in the data
3 Move to the next cell you want to work on – use any of the methods suggested

Moving around your datasheet

There are a number of ways to move from cell to cell within the Datasheet.

You can use the keys:

Arrow keys	one cell in direction of arrow
[Tab]	forward to the next cell
[Shift]-[Tab]	back to the previous cell
[Enter]	down to the next cell in a column

Or point to the cell and click

The cell you are in (your *current* cell) has a dark border.

Standard toolbar

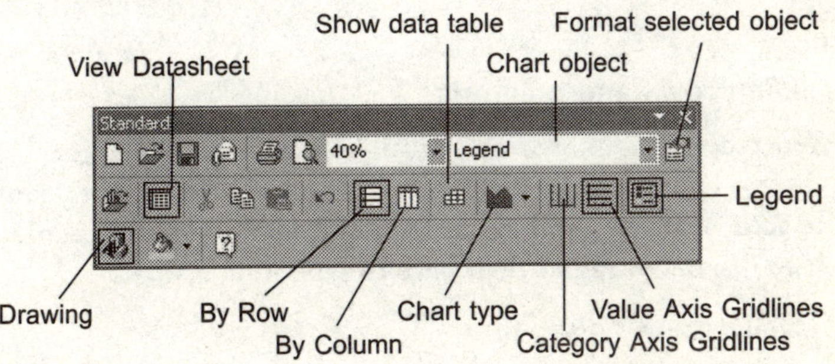

By Row or By Column

The **Category** axis has labels taken from the column or row headings in your datasheet. Use **By Row** and **By Column** on the Standard toolbar to indicate whether your data series is in rows or columns. A graphic in the row or column heading of your datasheet indicates the selected option.

Data series by row

Creatures of the Deep.ppt - Datasheet

		A	B	C	D	E
		Sharks	Whale	Dolphin	Walrus	
1	2000	78	55	82	60	
2	2001	88	62	75	56	
3	2002	110	70	89	58	
4						

The Value axis is the one your data is plotted against.

- Don't enter too much data – the chart will be seen on a slide or overhead. If it's too detailed your audience may not fully appreciate it.

View/hide datasheet

Once you have keyed in your data, you can hide the datasheet so you can see the chart clearly on your screen. If you hide your datasheet, you can easily view it again if you need to edit any data. Click the **View Datasheet** tool to view or hide the datasheet, as required.

Hiding rows and columns

You may have entered data into your datasheet, then decide that you don't wish to display it on the chart. If you don't want to actually delete the data, you can hide it. You can then unhide it to display it, rather than have to type it in again.

To hide a row or column:

1 Display the datasheet if necessary

2 Double-click on the column heading – the letter at the top of the column – you wish to hide

Or

3 Double-click the row number to the left of the row you wish to hide

The data is dimmed and will not appear on the chart. To reveal the data again double-click on the column heading or row number.

Formatting toolbar

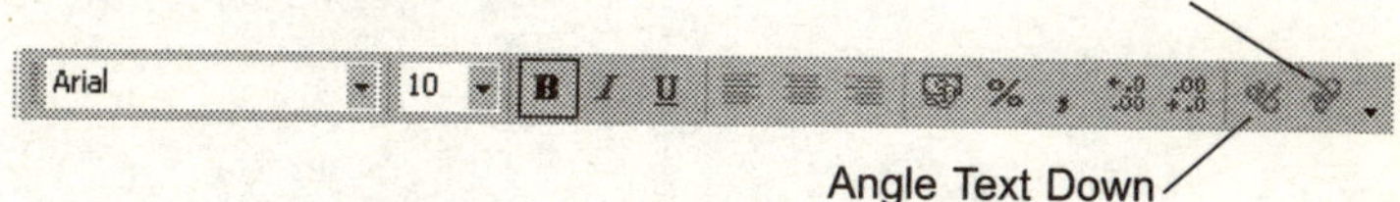

Number formats

Numbers can be displayed Currency, Percent or Comma styles.

Currency: £1,565.75 Percent: 156575%
Comma: 1,565.75

Select the cell(s), and click a style tool on the formatting toolbar.

5.3 Chart Type

A column chart is the default – the type used unless you specify a different one . You can try out a variety of other chart types using the Chart Type tool on the Standard toolbar.

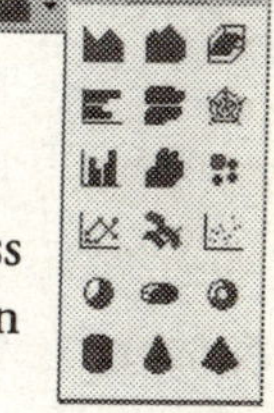

1 Click the drop-down arrow to display the chart types available

2 Choose one

Each chart type has a variety of sub-types. To access all the types and sub-types available you must open the **Chart Type** dialog box.

1 Open the **Chart** menu

2 Choose **Chart Type...**

3 Select the **Standard Types** tab

4 Explore the options available

5 Hold down the **Press and hold to View Sample** button to display a preview of your chart

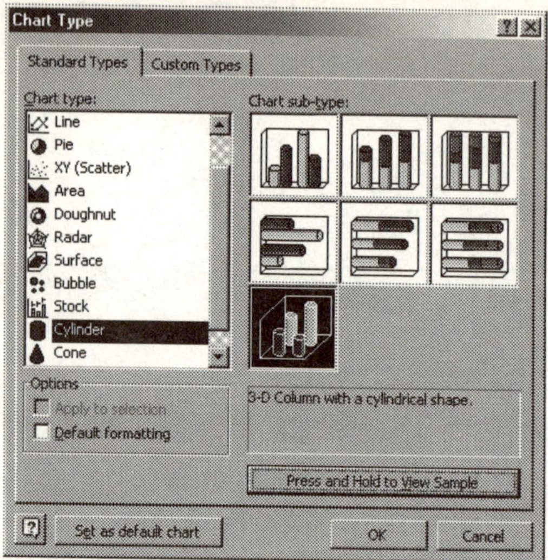

Changing the default chart type

If you do not normally use a column chart you can easily change the default chart type to the one that you use most often.

1 Select the chart type from the **Chart Type** dialog box

2 Click the **Set as default chart** button

3 Respond to the prompt asking if you are sure that you want to change the default chart type – click **Yes** if you are, **No** if you've changed your mind

- You'll find even more types to choose from on the **Custom Types** tab.

Adding your own custom chart type

If you have created a custom chart, e.g. a combination chart (see 5.6) or one with overlapping data series (see 5.7), and wish to reuse it, you can save it as a custom chart type.

1 Display the **Chart Type** dialog box

2 Select the **Custom Types** tab

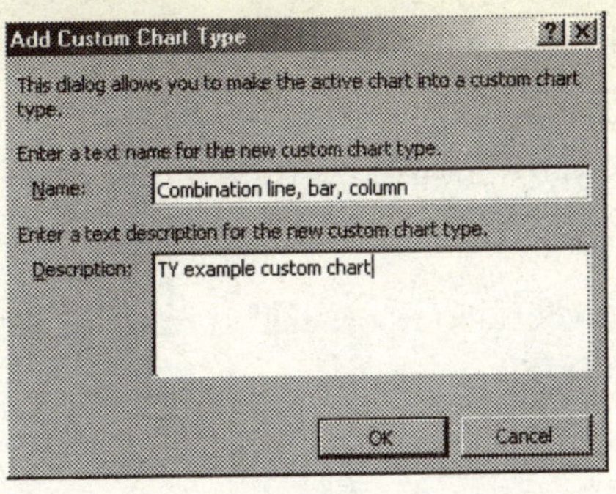

3 Click **Add...**

4 Give your chart a name and description (if you wish)

5 Click **OK**

- Combination charts are discussed later in the chapter.

5.4 Chart objects

Each part of your chart is an object in its own right. The chart objects are:

- Category axis
- Chart Area
- Corners
- Floor
- Legend
- Plot Area
- Value Axis
- Value Axis Major Grid Lines
- Walls
- Series

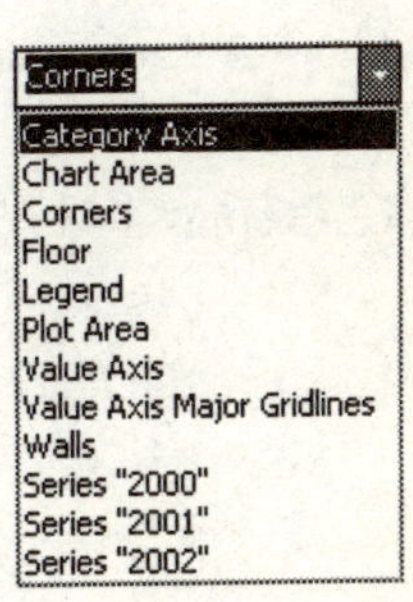

You can check where these objects are on your chart by using the **Chart Objects** tool. Select the object from the drop-down list, and have a look at your chart to see what has been selected – take a tour of the objects!

Formatting chart objects

You can format each object on your chart in a variety of ways. The formatting options vary from object to object.

To format an object:

1 Select it – click on it, or select it from the **Chart Object** list

2 Click the **Format** tool on the Standard toolbar

Or

- Double-click on the object that you wish to format

The **Format** dialog box for the object will be displayed. Explore the dialog box and experiment with its formatting options.

- The tools on the Formatting toolbar and Drawing toolbar can also be used to format the font size, font colour, alignment, fill colour, etc. of a selected object.

Try out the formatting suggested below to help get you started – then it's over to you to experiment!

Formatting the legend

The **Format Legend** dialog box contains many options for formatting this object, one of which is placement.

1 Display the **Format Legend** dialog box – double-click on the legend

2 Open the **Placement** tab

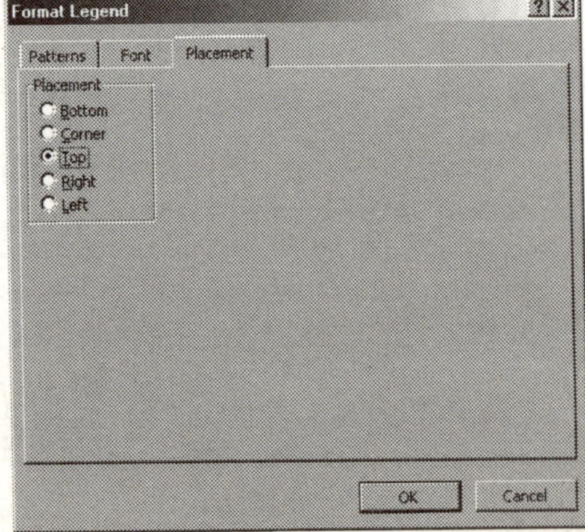

3 Choose the position that you require for the legend

4 Click **OK**

- Explore the **Patterns** and **Font** tabs to see what other options are available for this object.

5.5 Scale

By default, the scale on a graph starts at 0. In many graphs, you may not have any low values, in which case you will have a large 'dead' area on your chart where no points are plotted. You could change the scaling at times like this, so that the graph starts at a value closer to the points that will be plotted.

1 Display the **Format Axis** dialog box for the Value axis – double-click on the axis

2 Select the **Scale** tab

3 Set the **Minimum** value as required

4 Click **OK**

- Experiment with the other options in the dialog box and note their effect.

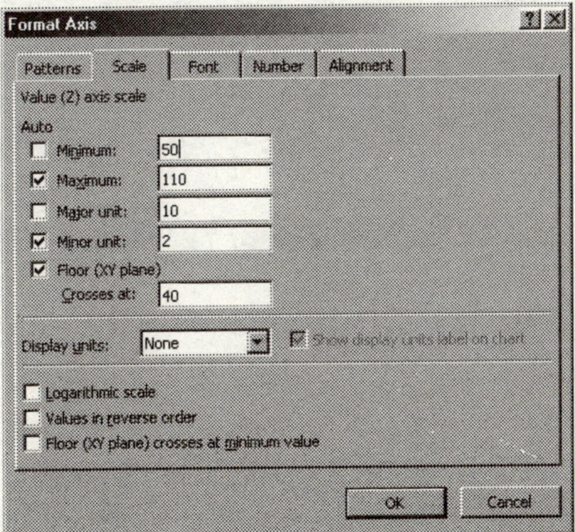

5.6 Combination charts

You can combine chart types on some 2-D charts. For example, you may want your chart to have most of the series displayed as a 2-D column chart, but want one series displayed as a line to add interest, and make the series stand out from the others. Column, bar and line charts can be combined.

To combine a column and line chart:

1 Display your chart as a 2-D column chart

2 Select the series that you wish to display as a line – click on it

3 Choose the **Line** option from the Chart types displayed when you click the down arrow at the **Chart Type** tool

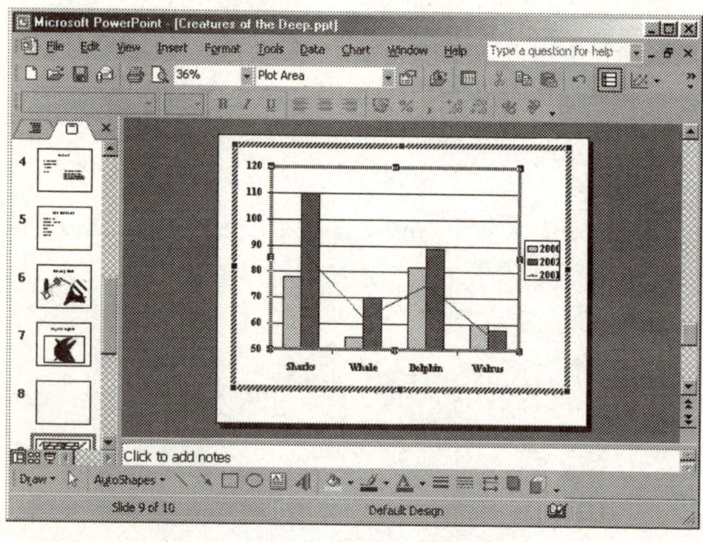

5.7 Overlap and Gap Width

The bars in a column or bar chart are displayed with no overlap between each series and a gap between each group. You can adjust the overlap and/or gap as required on your chart.

1 Display the **Format Data Series** dialog box – double-click on any data series

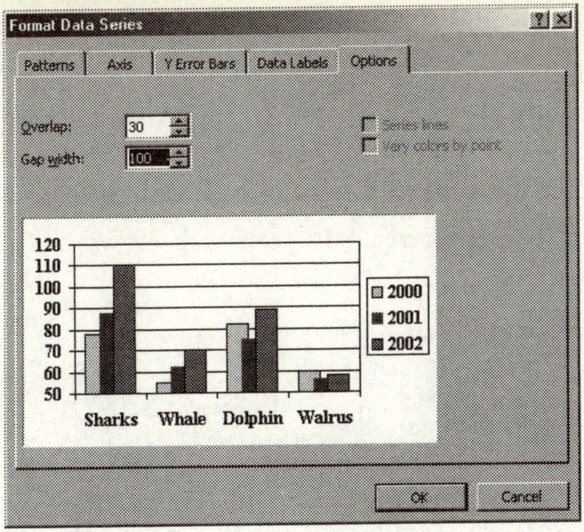

2 Select the **Options** tab
3 Edit the **Overlap** and **Gap width** fields to get the effects required
4 Click **OK**

5.8 Leaving Microsoft Graph

When your chart is complete, click anywhere on the slide outside the chart placeholder to return to your presentation.

The whole chart becomes an object within your presentation, and can be moved, copied, deleted or resized as necessary.

- To return to Microsoft Graph to edit your chart, simply double-click on the chart.

5.9 Importing a chart from Excel

If you use Excel, you may have created a chart in an Excel workbook that you wish to include in your presentation. You don't need to recreate the chart in PowerPoint, you can simply import it from Excel.

When you import a chart in this way, the whole workbook is inserted into your presentation.

1 Display the slide that you wish to display your chart on – a blank slide, or a slide with a title only is fine for this
2 Open the **Insert** menu and choose **Object**
3 Select **Create From File**, then click **Browse...** and locate your file

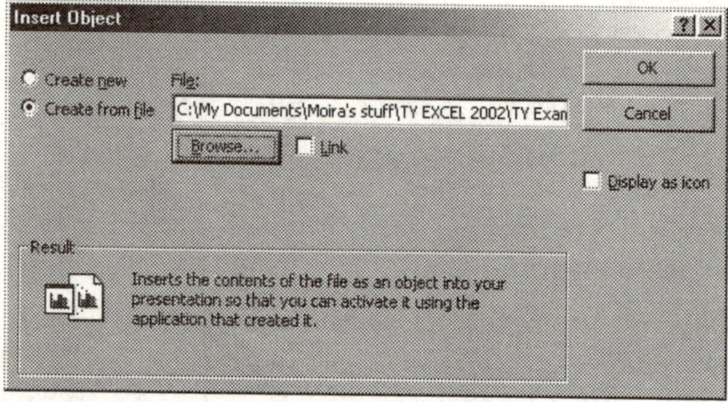

4 Click **OK** at the **Insert Object** dialog box

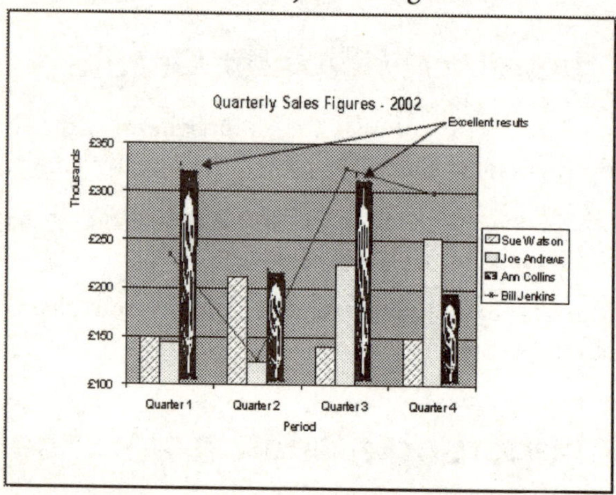

The whole workbook is inserted into your slide as an object. It is possible that the chart will not be visible, as it was not on the front-most sheet in the workbook.

If the chart you wish to display is not visible:

1 Double-click on the object to activate it
2 Select the sheet tab that contains your chart
3 Click outside the object to return to your presentation
4 Move and/or resize the object as necessary

Summary

In this chapter we have concentrated on creating charts on a slide. We have discussed:

- Creating a chart in PowerPoint
- Microsoft Graph toolbars and menus
- Entering data onto the datasheet
- Displaying data by row or by column
- Hiding data
- Number Formats
- Chart types
- Chart objects
- Formatting chart objects
- Scaling
- Combination charts
- Importing charts from Excel

In this chapter you will learn

- how to create organization charts
- what animation effects can be used on charts
- how to create diagrams
- how to AutoFormat a diagram

Aims of this chapter

This chapter introduces organization charts, which give you another opportunity to make your point using a diagram rather than words. We discuss creating organization charts on your slides, adding and removing boxes, layout, scaling options, formatting and animation. This chapter also looks at other diagrams – cycle, radical, pyramid, Venn and target.

6.1 Creating an organization chart

There are three main ways to set up an organization chart:

- Choose a layout with a **Diagram or Organization Chart** placeholder from the **Slide Layout** Task Pane

Or

- Choose a layout with a Content placeholder from the **Slide Layout** Task Pane

Or

- Click the **Insert Diagram or Organization Chart** tool

Using the Diagram or Organization Chart placeholder

1 Double-click in the placeholder on your slide

2 Select **Organization Chart** from the **Diagram Gallery** dialog box

3 Click **OK**

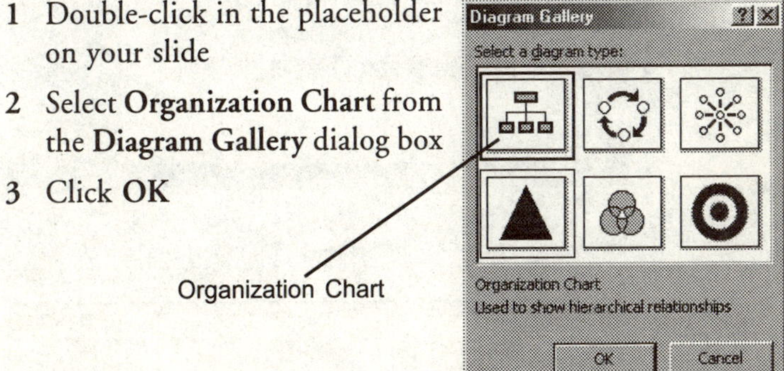

Using a Contents placeholder

1 Click the **Insert Diagram or Organization Chart** tool within the placeholder

2 Select **Organization Chart** from the **Diagram Gallery** dialog box

3 Click **OK**

Insert Diagram or Organization Chart

From a slide with no placeholder

1 Click the **Insert Diagram or Organization Chart** tool on the Drawing toolbar

2 Select **Organization Chart** from the **Diagram Gallery** dialog box

3 Click **OK**

An organization chart object will be displayed on your slide.

A set of boxes is displayed together with the Organization Chart toolbar.

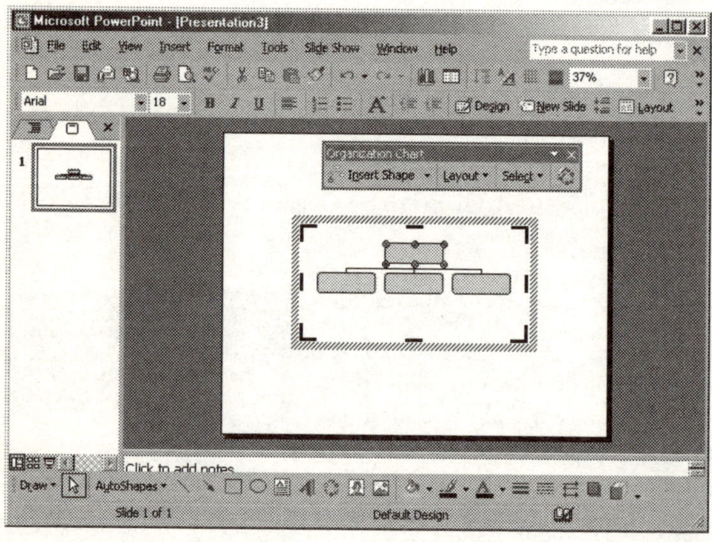

> **Tip**
>
> Work out the structure you wish to display before you start.
>
> Don't try to display too large a structure – the finished slide should be clear and easily understood

To enter your text:

1 Click in the box you wish to write in
2 Key in your data
3 Press [**Enter**] to create a new row if you have more than one line of data for the box
4 Click on the next box to be completed, or outside the box, when you are finished

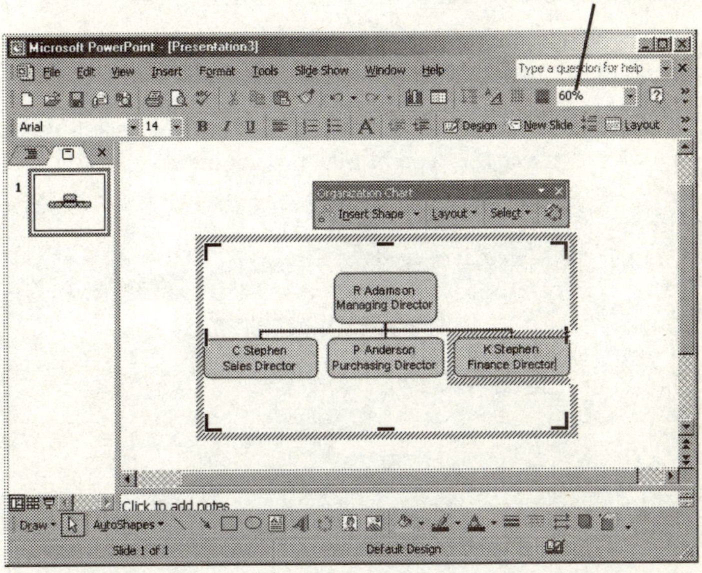

- If you click within the placeholder the Organization Chart toolbar remains visible. If you click outwith the placeholder the toolbar disappears. The toolbar will re-appear when you click inside the Organization Chart placeholder again.

6.2 Adding and deleting boxes

You can build your chart up by adding boxes. Each new box must be related to an existing box. There are three types of relationship – subordinate, co-worker and assistant.

To add a box:

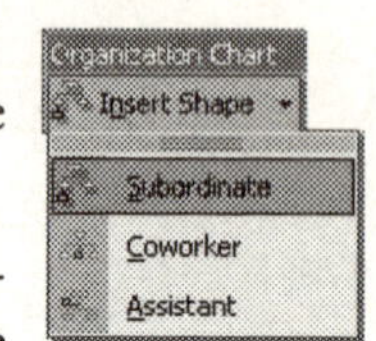

1 Click inside the box that you wish to relate a new box to

2 Click the **Insert Shape** tool on the Organization Chart toolbar to insert a Subordinate box (the default)

Or

3 Click the drop-down arrow to the right of the **Insert Shape** tool and select the type of new box required

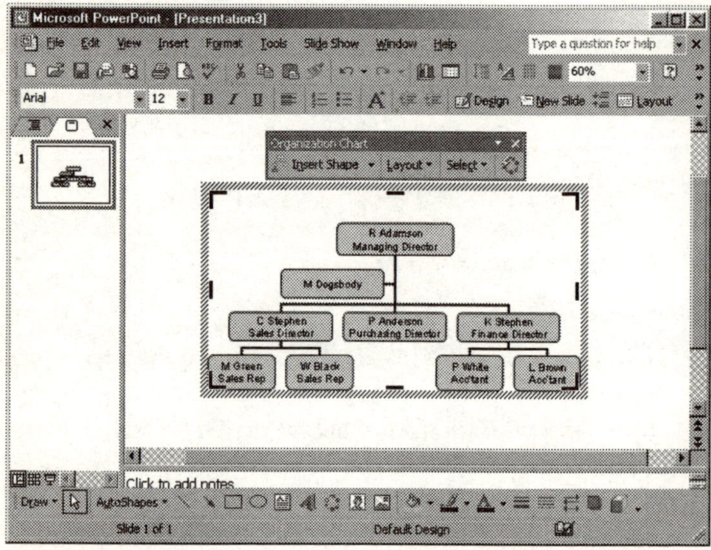

To delete a box:

1 Click in it, then click on its edge and press **[Delete]**

- If you change your mind, click **Undo** or press **[Ctrl]-[Z]** to undo the deletion.

6.3 Layout

There are a number of different layouts to choose from for your organization chart.

To change the layout:

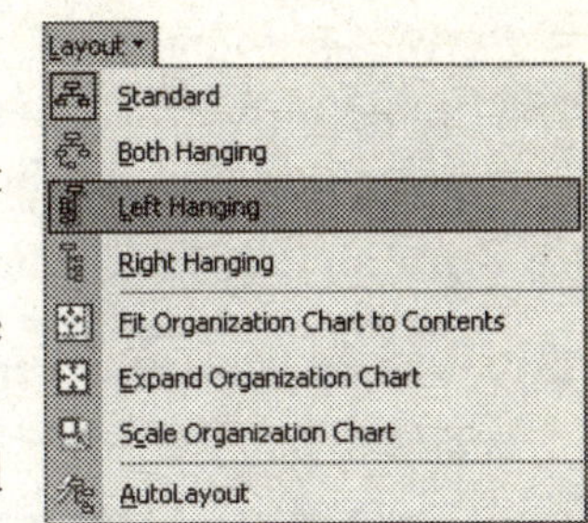

1 Select a 'manager' box – one that has subordinates
2 Click the **Layout** button on the Organization Chart toolbar
3 Select the layout option required

Fit/Expand/Scale

The **Layout** list also displays a number of options for controlling the size of the Organization Chart placeholder.

Fit Organization Chart to Contents

- Click this option if you want the organization chart placeholder border to fit snugly around the boxes.

Expand Organization Chart

- Use this tool to add space around the organization chart, within the placeholder

Scale Organization Chart

- If you select this option, handles appear in the corners and along the edges of the placeholder. Click and drag the handles to scale the chart as required.

Formatting the chart

You can format the chart manually, using the tools on the Formatting and Drawing toolbars (these options were discussed in Chapter 3 and 4).

To format a box or a line:

1 Select the object – click on it

2 Use the formatting tools on the Drawing toolbar, e.g. Line Style, Line Color, Fill, Shadow, etc.

To format text:

1 Select the text – drag over it
2 Use the formatting tools on the Formatting toolbar, e.g. Font size, Font color, Bold, Italic, etc.

To apply an AutoFormat to your chart:

1 Click the **AutoFormat** tool on the Organization Chart toolbar
2 At the Style Gallery, select the Diagram Style required
3 Click **Apply**

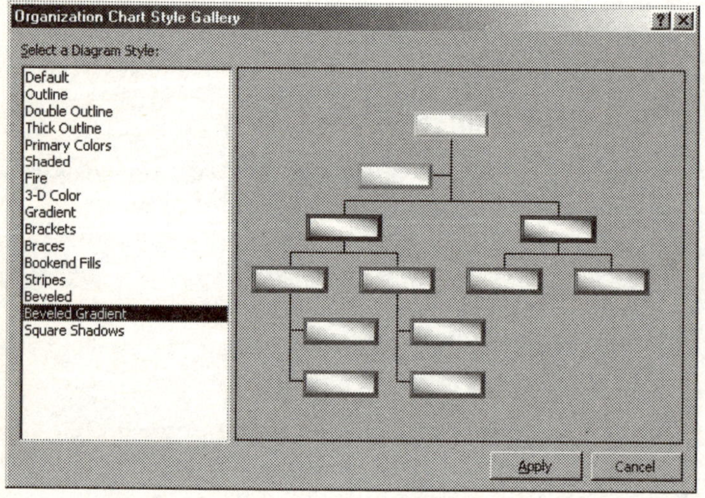

6.4 Animation

Animation can be used to create greater visual impact when your slide is displayed in a presentation.

To animate your organization chart:

1 Open the **Slide Show** menu
2 Choose **Custom Animation…**

3 The **Custom Animation** Task Pane will appear. Select the Organization Chart (if necessary)

4 Click **Add Effect...**

5 Choose the effect that you wish to use from the list

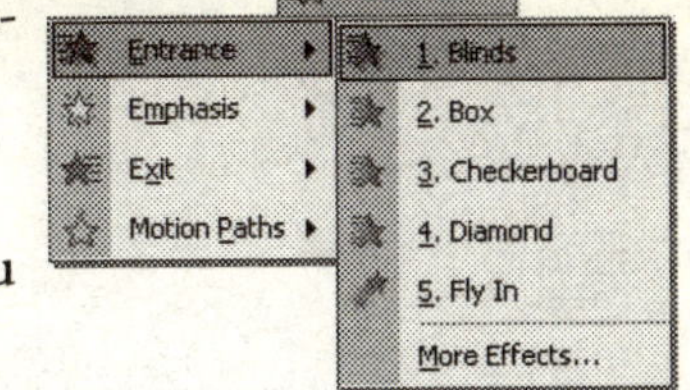

- Note the numbered tabs that appear on the slide in Normal view when the Custom Animation Task Pane is displayed. This indicates the order in which the animation will be carried out. The tabs do not appear in Slide Sorter or Slide Show view.

To change the animation effect:

1 Select the effect in the animation list on the Task Pane

2 Click the **Change** button

3 Select the effect required

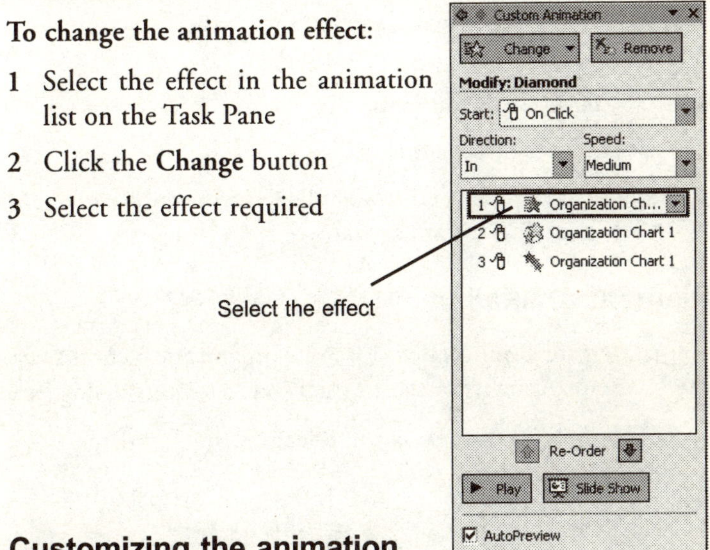

Customizing the animation

Once you have added an effect, you can use the fields in the **Custom Animation** Task Pane to customize the way the effect is executed.

Start

This option sets when the animation effect will start. There are three options – **On Click** (the one you are most likely to want), **With Previous** or **After Previous.**

On Click Starts the animation when you click the mouse
With Previous Starts at the same time as the previous item
After Previous Starts after the previous item has finished

Direction

The options vary, depending on the animation selected.

Speed

Select the speed that you think is best for your diagram.

Effect Options

You can further customize the effects from the **Effect Options** dialog box

1. Right-click on the animation effect on the Task Pane
2. Left-click on **Effect Options**
3. Explore the **Effect**, **Timing** and **Diagram Animation** tabs to see what options are available

Diagram Animation

You can create a build effect for your organization chart from the **Diagram Animation** tab in the **Effect Options** dialog box

1. Right-click on the animation effect on the Task Pane
2. Left-click on **Effect Options**
3. Select the **Diagram Animation** tab
4. Choose the option required from the **Group diagram** list
5. Click **OK**

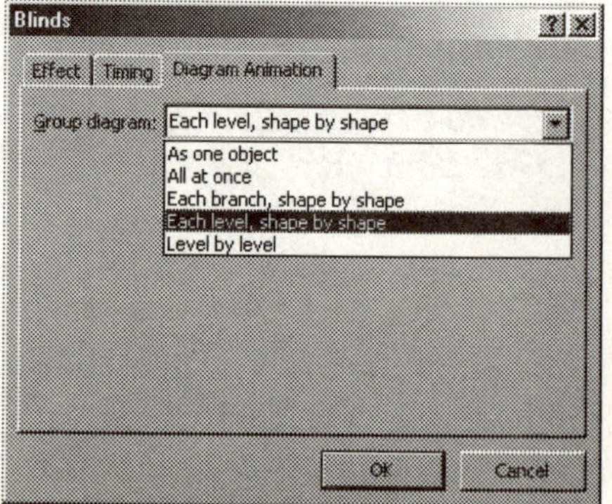

You can also customize the animation effect on each box within your organization chart – but be careful not to overdo things! Just because it is possible, doesn't necessarily mean that it is a good thing!

If you group the diagram using an option other than '**As one object**', you can customize the effects on individual boxes too!

To customize the effects on individual boxes:

1 Click the **Expand contents** bar to list the different boxes in your chart

2 Right-click the box that you wish to customize

3 Choose **Effect Options...** from the list

4 Customize the options as required

- Scroll to the bottom of the contents list and click the **Hide Contents** bar to collapse the contents list again.

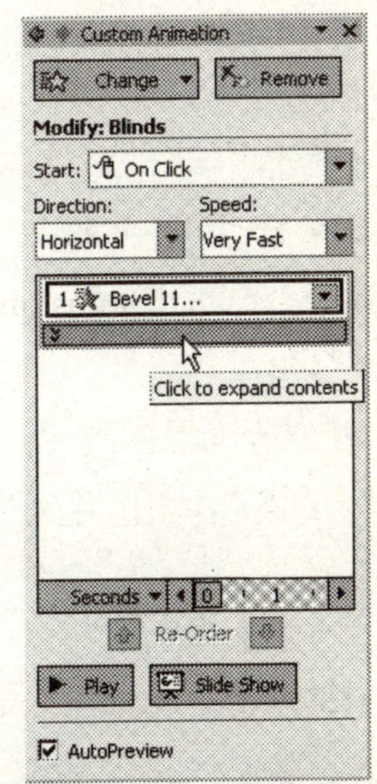

To remove an animation effect:

1 Select the effect on the list in the Task Pane.

2 Click the **Remove** button on the Task Pane.

6.5 Diagrams

Diagrams are used to represent conceptual data and to enliven your presentation.

You can add diagrams to your slides by creating a slide that has a Content placeholder on it, or by using the **Insert Diagram or Organization Chart** tool on the Drawing toolbar.

Creating a diagram

There are two main ways of creating a diagram:

- Choose a layout with a Content placeholder from the **Slide Layout** Task Pane

Or

- Click the **Insert Diagram or Organization Chart** tool

With a Content placeholder

1 Click the **Insert Diagram or Organization Chart** tool in the placeholder

Insert Diagram or Organization Chart

2 Select the diagram from the **Diagram Gallery** dialog box

3 Click **OK**

With no placeholder

1 Click the **Insert Diagram or Organization Chart** tool

2 Select the diagram from the **Diagram Gallery** dialog box

3 Click **OK**

Follow the prompts on the slide to complete your diagram.

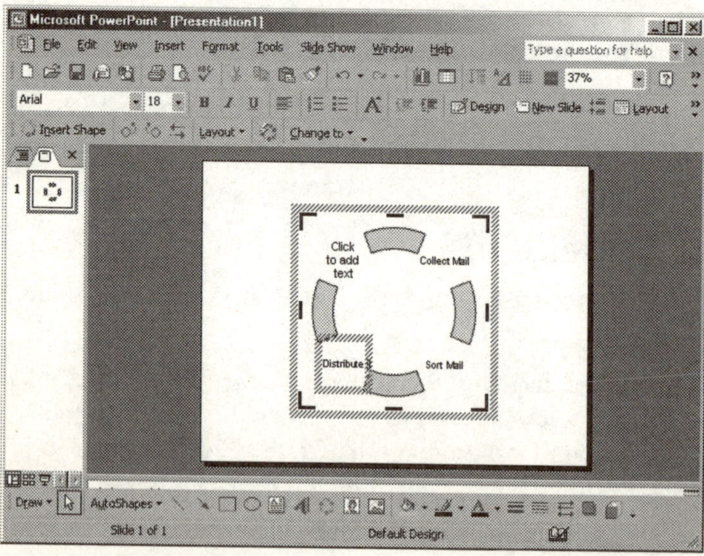

Diagram types

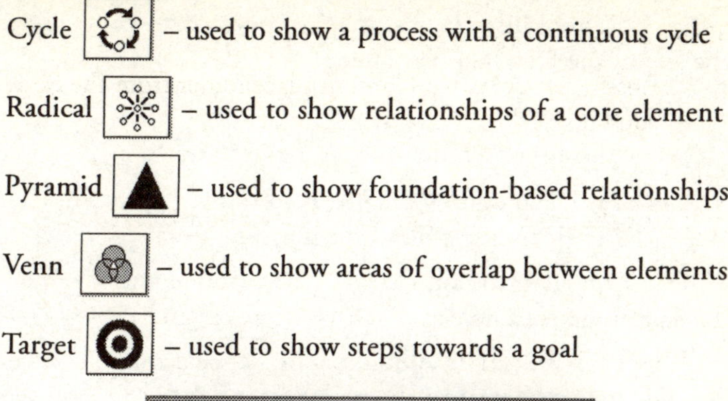

Cycle – used to show a process with a continuous cycle

Radical – used to show relationships of a core element

Pyramid – used to show foundation-based relationships

Venn – used to show areas of overlap between elements

Target – used to show steps towards a goal

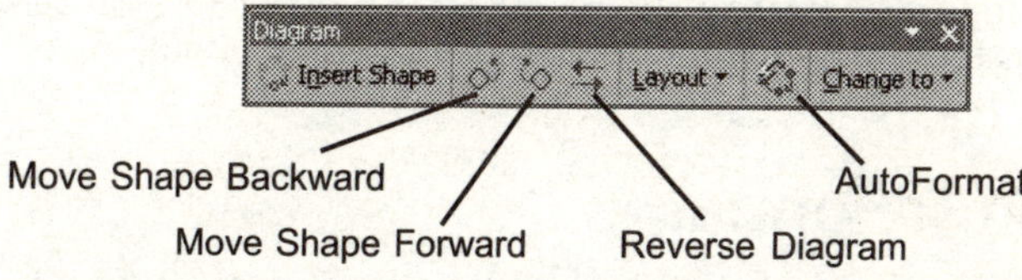

The Diagram toolbar is displayed when you are working on a diagram.

Use the toolbar to help you set up and format your diagram.

6.6 Working with shapes

You can easily add more shapes to your diagram.

To add a shape:

- Click the **Insert Shape** tool on the Diagram toolbar

To move a shape:

1 Select the shape

2 Click the **Move Shape Forward** or **Move Shape Backward** tool until the shape is in the required position

To delete a shape:

1 Right-click on it

2 Choose **Delete Shape** from the shortcut menu

To change the layout of the diagram

The Layout tool displays a number of options for controlling the size of the Diagram placeholder.

1 Click the **Layout** tool
2 Select the option required from the drop-down list

- Click **Fit Diagram to Contents** if you want the placeholder border to fit snugly around the diagram.
- Use **Expand Diagram** to add space around the diagram, within the placeholder
- If you select **Scale Diagram**, handles appear in the corners and along the edges of the placeholder. Click and drag the handles to scale the diagram as required.

6.7 AutoFormat

There are several AutoFormats to choose from that will help add impact to your diagram.

1 Click the **AutoFormat** tool
2 Choose a format option from the **Diagram Style Gallery**
3 Click **Apply**

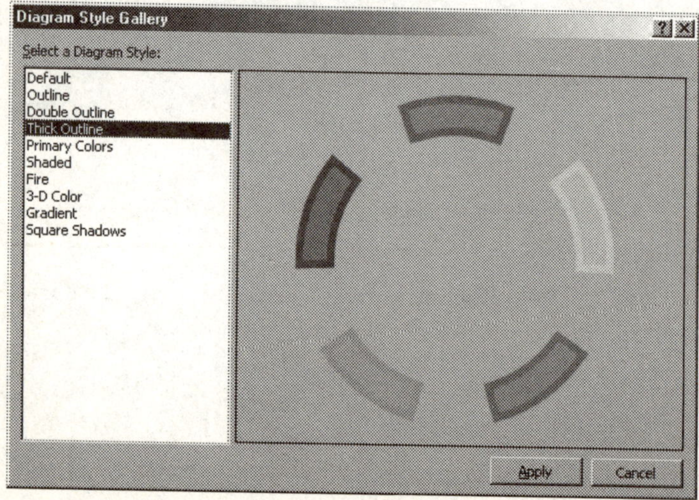

Changing the diagram type

If you decide that you would rather use a different type for your diagram, you can always change it.

1 Click the **Change To...** tool on the Diagram toolbar

2 Select the diagram type required from the list

- You can animate your diagrams using the same features as are available for organization charts.

Summary

In this chapter we have looked at organization charts and diagrams. We have discussed:

- Creating organization charts
- Adding and removing boxes
- Changing the layout of organization charts
- Scaling organization charts
- Formatting organization charts
- Animation in organization charts and other diagrams
- Creating diagrams – cycle, radical, pyramid, Venn and target
- Inserting, moving and deleting shapes
- Changing a diagram layout
- AutoFormatting diagrams
- Changing a diagram type

tables, clip art and sound

In this chapter you will learn

- how to create tables
- some ways of manipulating and formatting your tables
- about inserting and formatting ClipArt
- how to add sound effects

Aims of this chapter

In this chapter we will consider the use of tables, pictures and sounds on slides. Tables can display data in columns and rows. Pictures add interest to your slides, and sounds can help focus your audiences' attention on specific points.

7.1 Tables

If you have created tables in Word, you'll find it very easy to create thems on slides. A tables is inserted as an object and can be created in several ways. You can:

- Create a new slide with a Table placeholder set up
- Create a new slide with a Content placeholder
- *Draw* your table onto your slide
- Use the **Insert Table** tool on the Standard toolbar

To start from a slide with Table placeholder:

1 Double-click on the Table placeholder on your slide
2 Set the number of columns and rows
3 Click **OK**

To start from a slide with a Content placeholder:

1 Click the **Insert Table** tool within the placeholder
2 Specify the number of rows and column required
3 Click **OK**

The Tables and Borders toolbar

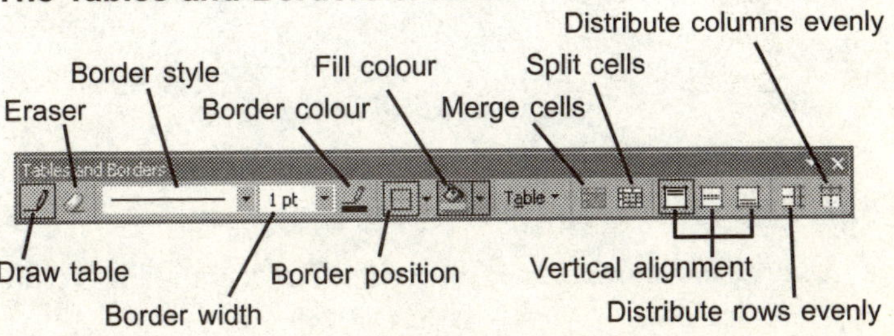

To draw a table:

1 Click the **Tables and Borders** tool on the Standard toolbar to display the **Tables and Borders** toolbar

2 The **Draw Table** tool is automatically selected (if you had the Tables and Borders toolbar displayed already, click the **Draw Table** tool to select it).

3 Click and drag on your slide to draw a rectangle the size you want your table to be

4 Draw in rows and columns where you want them

5 Switch the **Draw Table** tool off – click or press [**Esc**]

If you draw a line in the wrong place, remove it with the **Eraser** – select the tool , then click on the line you wish to erase with the tip of the Eraser.

From a slide with no Table placeholder set up:

1 Click on the **Insert Table** tool on the Standard toolbar

2 Click and drag over the grid to specify the table size required

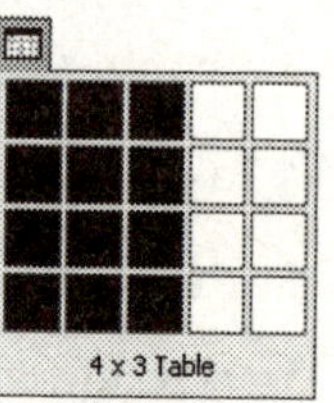

When working in a table:

- Press [**Tab**] to move to the next cell
- Press [**Shift**]-[**Tab**] to go to the previous cell

Or

- Use the arrow keys to move up, down, right and left

Or

- Click in the cell you wish to work on.

Click outside your table when you've finished working on it (the Tables and Borders toolbar will disappear).

- Use the **Formatting** and **Tables and Borders** toolbars to format your data.

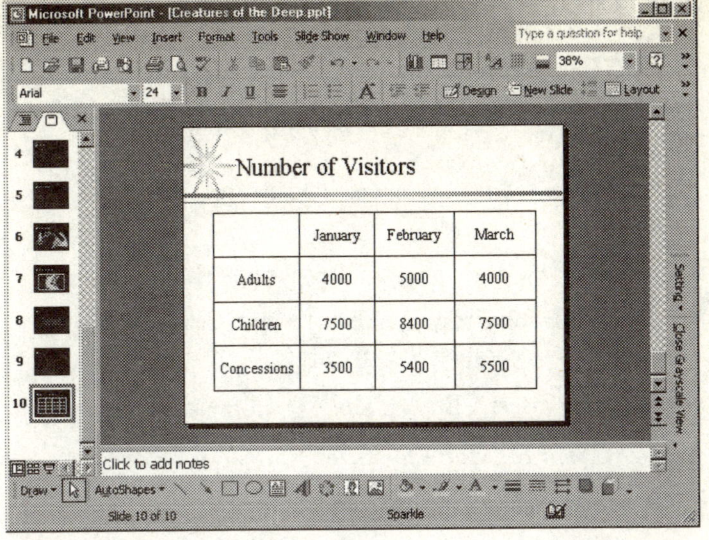

Tips when working with tables

- **To select table cells**: drag over them
- **To adjust a column width**: drag the left column border
- **To adjust a row height**: drag the lower row border
- **To insert or delete a row or column:** click on the **Table** button on the Tables and Borders toolbar, then left-click on the option (you will need to adjust the column width/ row height manually to get a good fit).
- To resize rows and/or columns so that they are the same height/ width, select them, then use **Distribute Rows Evenly** or **Distribute Columns Evenly** tools.

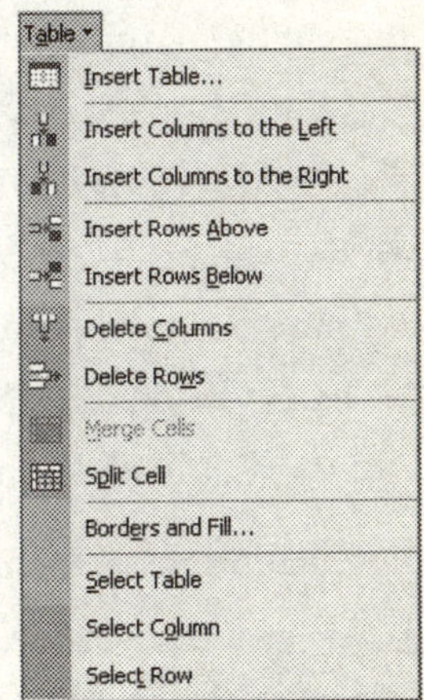

7.2 Clip art

Office XP comes with 100s of clip art pictures that can be added to slides. You can also find many more clips on the Internet.

There are four main ways of getting your hands (or mouse) on the clip art.

- Set up a New Slide with a **Clip Art** placeholder on it
- Choose a layout from the **Slide Layout** Task Pane that has a Content placeholder already on it
- Click the **Insert Clip Art** tool on the Drawing toolbar
- Insert from the Clip Organizer

From a slide with a Clip Art placeholder:

- Double click within the Clip Art placeholder

From a slide with a Content placeholder:

- Click the **Insert Clip Art** tool within the Content placeholder

Both of these options take you to the **Select Picture** dialog box.

To select a picture:

1 Scroll through the pictures, and then select the one that you want and click **OK**

Or

2 Enter a keyword into the **Search** field and click **Search**

3 Select the picture that you want to use and click **OK**

From a slide with no placeholder set:

1 Click the **Insert Clip Art** tool on the Drawing toolbar

2 At the **Insert Clip Art** Task Pane, enter a keyword, e.g. *animal* in the **Search text:** field

3 Set your search options

4 Click **Search**

- If you don't enter a keyword, all available clips will be displayed

If you don't find anything suitable, click **Modify** at the bottom of the Task Pane and try another keyword (or leave the **Search text:** field empty, and scroll through all the clips to see what is available).

7.3 Clip Organizer

You could also have a browse through the Clip Organizer.

1 Click **Clip Organizer** at the bottom of the **Insert Clip Art** Task Pane

2 Display the **Collection List** pane

3 Explore the **Collections** folders until you locate a clip that you want to use

4 Click the drop-down arrow to the right of the clip

5 Select **Copy**

6 Return to your slide and click the **Paste** tool

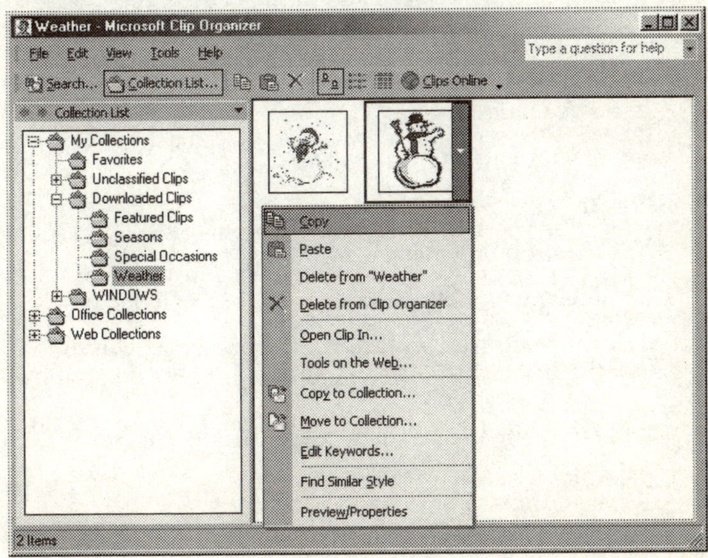

Organizing your clips

You can add and delete clips from the Clip Organizer. You can also move clips and edit the keywords.

To add clips:

If you have clips on your hard disk that are not displayed in the organizer…

1 Display the Clip Organizer dialog box
2 From the **File** menu choose **Add Clips to Organizer**
3 Choose **Automatically** – your disk will be scanned for clips and they'll be added to the organizer 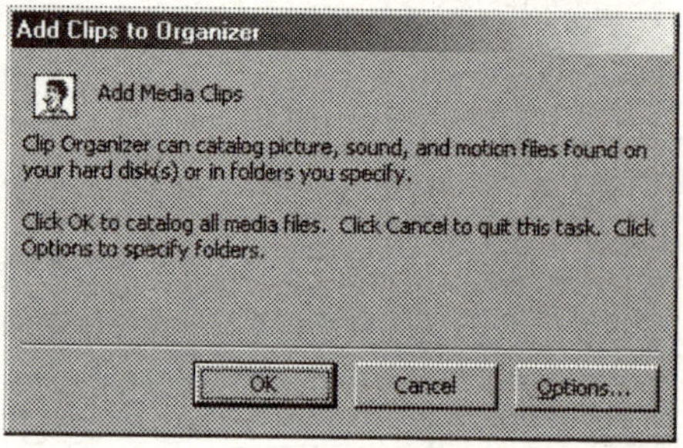
4 Click **OK** to scan all folders, or click **Options…** to specify which folders you want scanned

To delete a clip:

1 Select it in the Clip Organizer
2 Click the drop-down arrow to the right of the clip
3 Choose **Delete from** ***folder name*** or **Delete from Clip Organiser** as required

To copy or move a clip:

1 Select the clip you wish to move
2 Click the drop-down arrow to the right of the clip
3 Choose **Copy to Collection…** or **Move to Collection…**
4 Select the folder you wish to copy or move the clip to

Or

5 Click **New…** to create a new folder for the clip
6 Click **OK**

To edit the keywords:

When you search for a clip, the clips that have the keyword you have specified in the search are displayed. You can edit the clips' keywords if necessary

1 Select the clip that you want to edit the keyword(s) for

2 Click the drop-down arrow to the right of the clip

3 Select **Edit Keywords…**

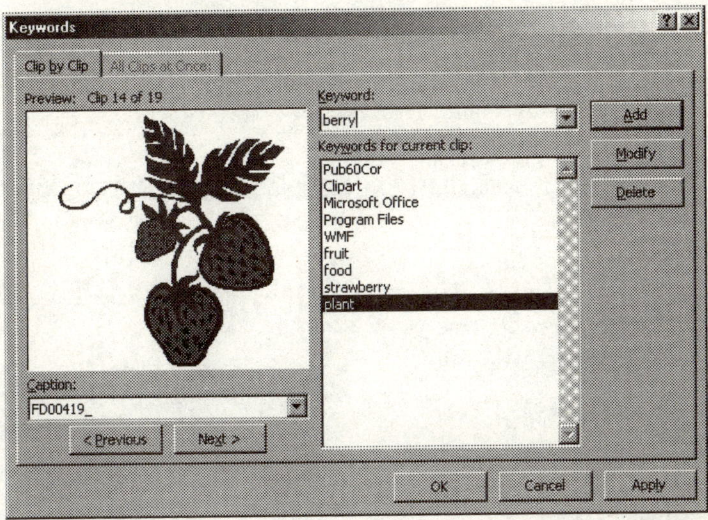

To add a keyword:

1 Type the word into the **Keyword** field

2 Click **Add**

To modify a keyword:

1 Select the word from the list

2 Type in the modified entry

3 Click **Modify**

To delete a keyword:

1 Select it from the list

2 Click **Delete**

Clips online

If you have access to the Internet you will find hundreds of clips online.

1 Click **Clips Online** at the bottom of the **Insert Clip Art** Task Pane

2 Read and accept the *License agreement* when it appears

3 Explore the online clips

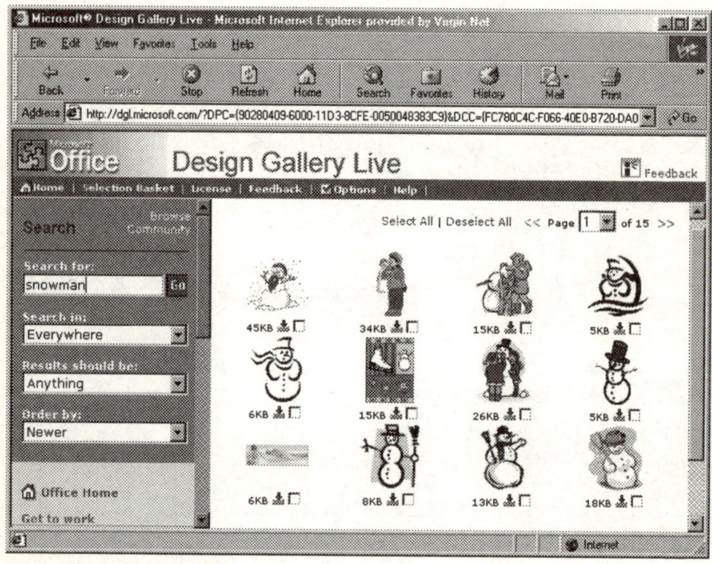

To search for a clip:

1 Specify your search options in the panel on the left

2 Click **Go**

3 Move through the pages using the right/left arrows

4 Click on a clip to preview it

5 Click the download button under the clip to copy it to your computer
6 Click **Accept** at the licence agreement
7 Click **Download now**
8 The clip will be displayed in the Downloaded Clips collections in the Clip Organizer

To copy the clip onto your slide:

1 Click the drop-down arrow to the right of the clip
2 Click on **Copy**
3 Return to your presentation and paste the clip onto the slide
4 Resize and move as required
5 Close the Clip Organizer dialog box

Formatting clips

The picture can be edited in the same way as other objects.

After you have clicked on a picture to select it, you can…

- Press [**Delete**] to delete the object
- Click and drag any of the handles around the edges of the picture to resize it
- Click and drag within the picture (not a handle) to move it
- Use the **Picture** toolbar to create special effects

Deselect it by clicking anywhere off it

The Picture toolbar

The clips that you insert into your document can be formatted in a number of ways – the best thing to do is experiment with the options and see what effect they have.

When a clip is selected the Picture toolbar is displayed. You can use the toolbar to modify your picture.

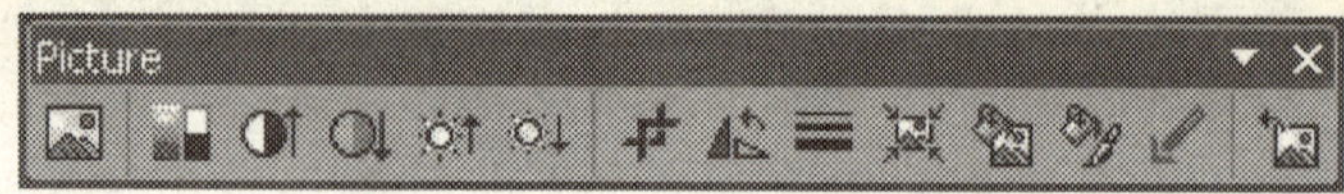

Working from left to right on the toolbar:

Insert Picture – Inserts a picture *from File* rather than from the **Clip Organizer** or **Select Picture** dialog box

Color – Automatic is the default. Grayscale converts each colour to a different shade of grey. Black and white converts the picture to a black and white picture. Watermark converts the object to a low contrast picture that you can place behind everything else to create a watermark.

More Contrast – Increase the contrast

Less Contrast – Decrease the contrast

More Brightness – Increase the brightness

Less Brightness – Decrease the brightness

Crop – Lets you trim the edges of the clip

To crop a clip:

1 Select it
2 Click the **Crop** tool
3 Drag a resizing handle to crop (cut off) the bits you don't want

Rotate Left – Rotates the object 90° to the left

Line Style – Use to put lines around the picture, or change the line style used

Compress Pictures – Displays a dialog box which displays options for reducing the picture's file size

Recolor picture – Displays a dialog box where you can change the colours used a picture

Format Picture – Opens the Format Picture dialog box where you have access to even more formatting options

Set Transparent Color – Used to integrate a picture on your page. For bitmaps, JPEGs and GIFs that don't have transparency information, and also some clip art

Reset Picture – returns the clip to its original state

7.4 Sound

You can add sound to your slides from the **Media Clip** dialog box or the Clip Organizer.

To add sound from the Media Clip dialog box:

1 Create a layout with a Media Clip or a Content placeholder

2 Double-click the **Media Clip** placeholder

Or

- Click the **Insert Media Clip** tool in the Content placeholder

3 Select the clip you wish to add (sound or video clip)

4 Click **OK**

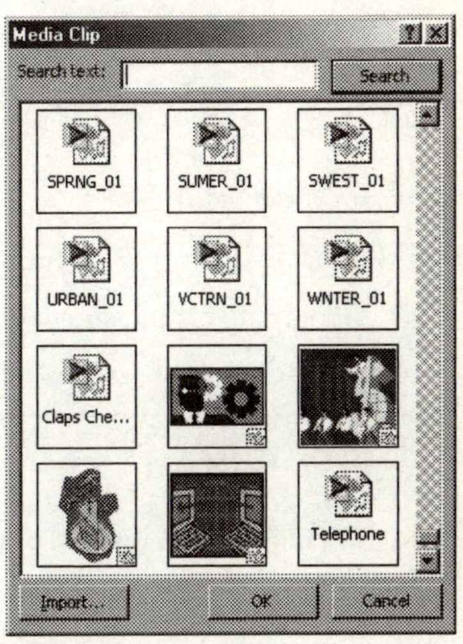

To add a sound from the Clip Organizer:

1 Display the Clip Organizer dialog box

2 Locate a folder that contains sounds

3 Select the sound

4 Right-click on the drop-down arrow to the right of the clip

5 Select **Copy**

6 Return to your slide

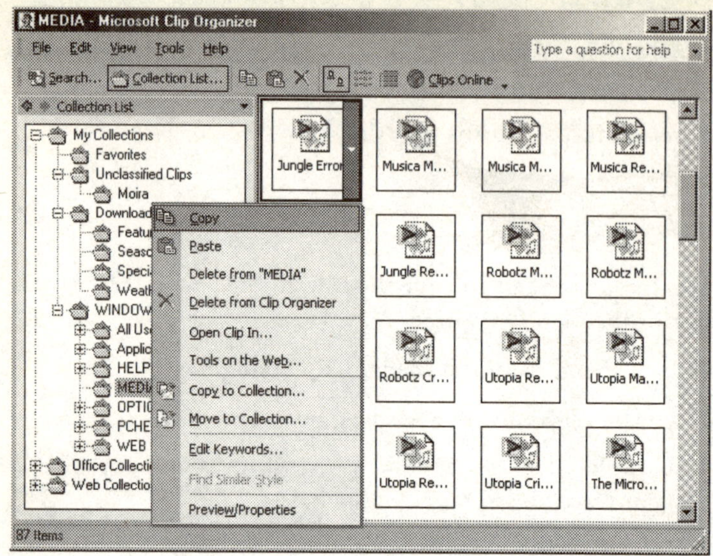

7 Paste the clip in

8 Move/resize the clip as required

- When giving a slide show, click on the sound icon to play it

Summary

In this chapter we have discussed:

- Tables for displaying columns and rows of data
- Clip art to illustrate a point or add interest to a slide
- Sound – don't overdo this – but it can be effective!

08 masters

In this chapter you will learn

- about Master slides
- how to add headers and footers
- about Handout and Notes masters

Aims of this chapter

This chapter discusses Masters. Each presentation is based on a design template which consists of a slide master, title master (optional), and the various styles for the presentation, e.g. font styles, placeholder sizes and positions, background design, colour scheme, etc. Masters are used as the pattern for the slides in your presentation. If you wish to make a layout or formatting change that will be reflected on all slides (or all title slides), you should update the appropriate master. There are also masters for handouts and notes pages.

8.1 Slide Master

A Slide Master is added to a presentation any time you apply a design template. Most design templates have a Slide Master and a Title Master – the Slide-Title Master pair. These are displayed as miniatures in the slide panel when you view a master.

Any background objects you want to appear on every slide (e.g. a company name or logo) should be added to the Slide Master.

Changes to the Slide Master will be reflected in every slide in your presentation (except the Title Slide). Any slides where you have made changes to the text formatting at slide level will be treated as exceptions and will retain their custom formatting.

To access the master slides:

1 Choose **Master** from the **View** menu

2 Select **Slide Master**

3 Amend the Slide Master as required (using the same techniques you use on a slide in your presentation)

4 Click the **Close Master View** tool or choose an alternative view to leave your Slide Master

- If you hold down [**Shift**] and click the **Normal View** icon ▣, this takes you to the Slide Master or to the Title Master if you are on the title slide at the time.

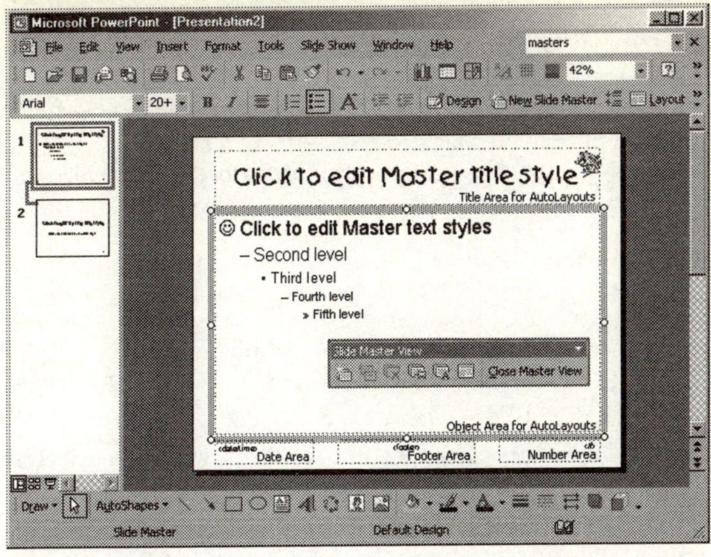

- The title slide has its own master. Changes made to the Slide Master will not be reflected on your Title slide.

The Slide Master View toolbar

From left to right:

Insert New Slide Master adds a new Slide Master to your presentation – each presentation must have at least one Slide Master

Insert New Title Master adds a new Title Master to your presentation

Delete Master deletes the selected Master

Preserve Master protects the Master from being deleted automatically by PowerPoint.

When all the slides that follow a master are deleted, or when another template is applied to all the slides that follow a Master, PowerPoint usually automatically deletes the Slide

Master. If you don't want this to happen, you can 'preserve' a Master so it isn't automatically deleted.

- Click the **Preserve Master** tool to toggle the preserve status on Masters.
- A Master can be deleted manually even when it has a 'preserved' setting.

Rename Master opens a dialog box where you can rename the Master

Master Layout displays the Master Layout dialog box, where you can switch on any placeholders that you have deleted from the master

Close Master View returns you to the view you were in before accessing the Masters

The placeholders

The Object Areas for AutoLayouts, Date Area, Footer Area or Number Area placeholders are all optional. They can easily be deleted – or put back if you decide you want them after all.

You can delete any of the master placeholders – if you don't want to use them.

To delete placeholder:

- Select the placeholder and press **[Delete]**

To restore placeholders:

1 Click the **Master Layout** tool on the **Slide Master View** toolbar

2 Select the placeholders required

3 Click **OK**

Multiple Masters

If a presentation uses more than one design template, e.g. a different template for different sections of the presentation, you will have more than one set of masters. The Slide Master toolbar has a set of tools that can be used when working with multiple slide masters – tools for adding, deleting, renaming and preserving slide masters.

8.2 Headers and Footers

You can control the date options, switch on slide numbering, or enter text for the footer area in the **Header and Footer** dialog box. You can access this dialog box in Normal view or in Master view.

1 Open the **View** menu and choose **Header and Footer**
2 Select the **Slide** tab
3 Complete the dialog box as required
4 Click **Apply to All** or **Apply**

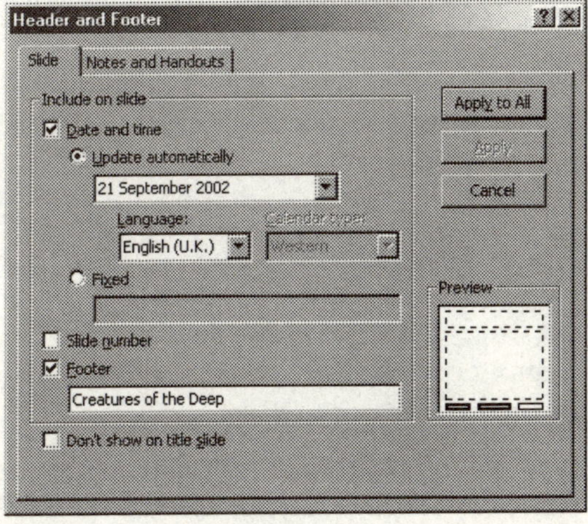

8.3 Handout Master

You can support your presentation with audience handouts if you wish. Handouts consist of smaller, printed versions of your slides, 1, 2, 3, 4, 6 or 9 to the page.

If you want additional information on each handout page, e.g. your company name or logo, the presentation title, page numbers or date, you can add the detail to the Handout Master.

To edit the Handout Master:

1 Choose **Master** from the **View** menu

2 Select **Handout Master**

3 Select 1, 2, 3, 6 or 9 slides to the page

4 Edit the Master as required

5 To edit the header and/or footer choose **Header and Footer** from the **View** menu and select the Notes and Handouts tab

6 Edit the header and/or footer text and click **Apply to All**

7 Click **Close Master View** or choose an alternative view to leave your Handout Master

- You can view the Handout Master if you hold down [**Shift**] and click the Slide Sorter View icon
- The 3 slides to a page layout is particularly useful if you want to leave space for your audience to make their own notes beside each slide

8.4 Notes Master

Each slide in your presentation has an accompanying notes page which consists of a smaller version of the slide along with room for any notes you want to make.

If you want to add information to your notes pages (company name or page number perhaps), or change the size of the placeholders (to allow more space for notes and less for the slide image) do so on the Notes Master.

1 Choose **Master** from the **View** menu

2 Select **Notes Master**

3 Amend the Notes Master as required

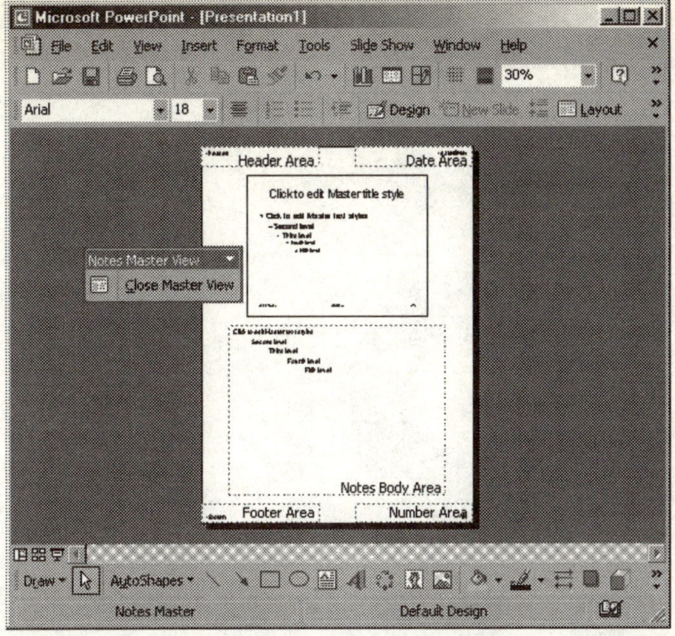

4 Click **Close Master View** or choose an alternative view to leave your Notes Master

Summary

In this chapter we have discussed the masters that are part of the design template of a presentation.

- The masters control the size and position of the placeholders on your slides
- Masters hold the design elements of a presentation, e.g. colour schemes, font and font size, bullet style, etc.
- Global changes to slides should be made on the slide master, and to title slides on the title slide master
- Objects on the masters appear on every slide or page
- The masters can be displayed by holding the [Shift] key down when you click a View icon

slide show preparation

In this chapter you will learn

- how to prepare a slide show
- how to create a summary slide
- how to create speaker notes
- about transitions and animation
- some ways of customizing the show setup

Aims of this chapter

Slide Sorter view was mentioned in Chapter 3 where we considered how you could move or copy slides. There are several other useful features worth exploring in Slide Sorter view that can help you prepare for your slide show, including:

- Hiding slides
- Setting up transitions
- Animating text on slides
- Rehearsing timings

We'll look at these features in this chapter, and see how they can help enhance your presentations.

You should be in Slide Sorter view for this chapter.

9.1 Slide Sorter toolbar

- The topics introduced in this section are useful if you will be giving on-screen presentations (a slide show). They do not apply to overheads and 35mm slides.
- Transitions, Text Animation and Hiding Slides can be specified in any view using the Tools menu, but I find it easiest to do them from Slide Sorter view using the Slide Sorter toolbar.

Hide Slide

This option can prove useful if you're not sure whether or not you will really need a particular slide for your presentation. You can include the slide in your presentation (in case it's needed), but hide it. The hidden slide will be by-passed during your slide show, unless you decide you need to use it.

To hide a slide:

1 Select the slide you want to hide

2 Click the **Hide Slide** tool

- The number is crossed out under the slide

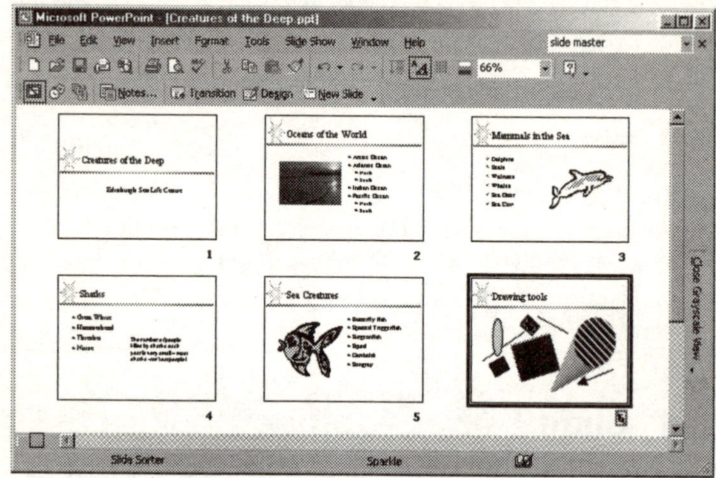

- If you want to show the hidden slide during a presentation press [H] at the slide preceding the hidden one.
- To remove the hidden status from a slide, select it and click the **Hide Slide** tool again.

9.2 Rehearse timings

It is a very good idea to practise your presentation before you end up in front of your audience. As well as practising what you intend to say (probably with the aid of notes you have made using the Notes Pages feature), you can rehearse the timings for each slide.

1 Click the **Rehearse Timings** tool to go into your slide show for a practice run!

2 Go over what you intend to say while the slide is displayed

Slide time
Pause
Repeat
Presentation time
Next
Rehearsal
0:00:03
0:01:11

3 Click the left mouse button to move to the next slide when ready

4 Repeat steps 2 and 3 until you reach the end of your presentation

Displaying timings

A dialog box displays the total length of time your presentation took and asks if you want to record and use the new slide timings in a slide show. Choose **Yes**, if you want each slide to advance after the allocated time.

The slide timings will be displayed in Slide Sorter view.

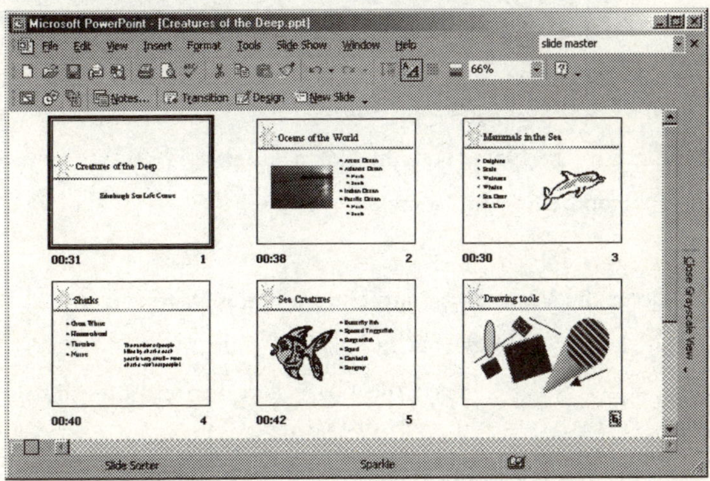

- You can rehearse your timings as often as is necessary, until you've got the pace right to get your message across.

- You can set your timings manually in the **Slide Transition** Task Pane.

9.3 Summary Slide

You can get PowerPoint to automatically produce a Summary Slide for your presentation. This will be placed in front of the other slides, and list the title of each slide.

To create a summary slide:

1 Hold [**Shift**] and click to select the slides from which you wish to produce a Summary Slide.

2 Click the **Summary Slide** tool on the Slide Sorter toolbar

- PowerPoint will generate as many Summary Slides as is necessary to list the title detail from all the slides you select.

9.4 Speaker Notes

If you are giving the presentation, you will probably find Speaker Notes useful. You can print your notes out, and use them to prompt you during your talk.

To enter and edit Speaker Notes:

1 Click in the Notes Pane in Normal view

2 Type and edit your notes

Or

1 Open the **View** menu and choose **Notes Page**

2 Click in the Notes area and type in your notes

(You may want to increase the Zoom if you enter notes in this view, so that you can read your text).

You can also input and edit your notes in Slide Show view. This option may be particularly useful when you a practising your show.

1 Select the slide that you wish to update the notes of

2 Click the **Speaker Notes** tool to view/edit the notes for the selected slide.

3 Enter/edit the notes as required

4 Click **Close**

9.5 Transition

A transition is an effect used between slides in a show. The default option is that no transition is set, but there are several interesting alternatives that you might find effective for your presentation. Experiment with the transition options until you discover those best suited to your presentation.

To set a transition:

1 Select the slide(s) to which you want to specify a transition

2 Click the **Slide Transition** tool

- The **Slide Transition** Task Pane is displayed.

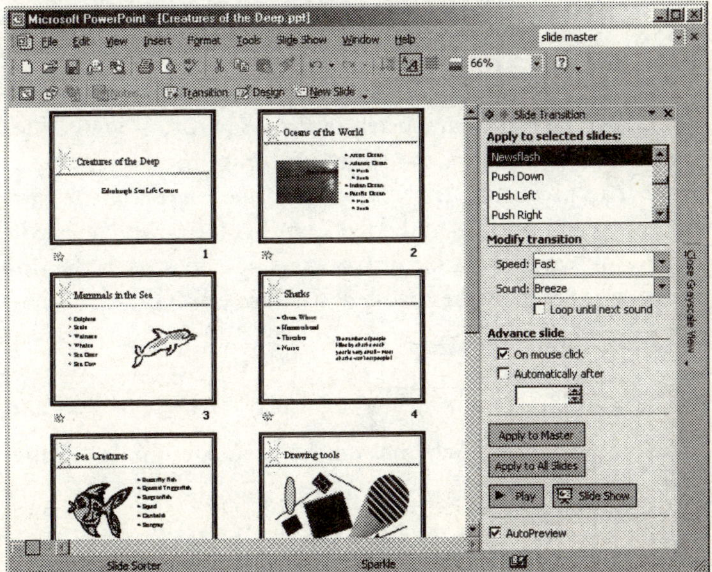

3 Select the effect required from the list (it will be previewed if **AutoPreview** is selected at the bottom of the Task Pane).
4 Set the **Speed** to *Fast*. Focus your audiences on your slides, not the transition method!
5 Select a **Sound** if you wish
6 Choose an **Advance** option

Other options

- **Apply to Master** saves the effect in the slide master. All new slides added to the presentation will have the transition effect.
- **Apply to All** applies the effect to all slides in the presentation, not just the one(s) you have selected. New slides will not have the transition effect.
- **Play** previews the effect on the selected slide.
- **Slide Show** displays the slide and effect in Slide Show view.

If a transition is set, a transition icon appears below the slide in Slide Sorter view. Click on it to see the effect.

9.6 Animation

If you have several points listed in the body text of your slide, you could try building the slide up during the presentation, rather than presenting the whole list at once. Experiment with the Animation options and effects until you find the ones you prefer. You can have a lot of fun messing about with the options – but try to avoid having a different effect on each slide!

To set an animation effect:

1 Click the **Design** tool Design to display the **Design** Task Pane
2 Select **Animation Schemes** on the **Slide Design** Task Pane
3 Select the slide(s) that you wish to animate
4 Pick an effect from the list

5 Click **Apply to Master** or **Apply to All Slides**

6 Close the Pane when you have specified your requirements

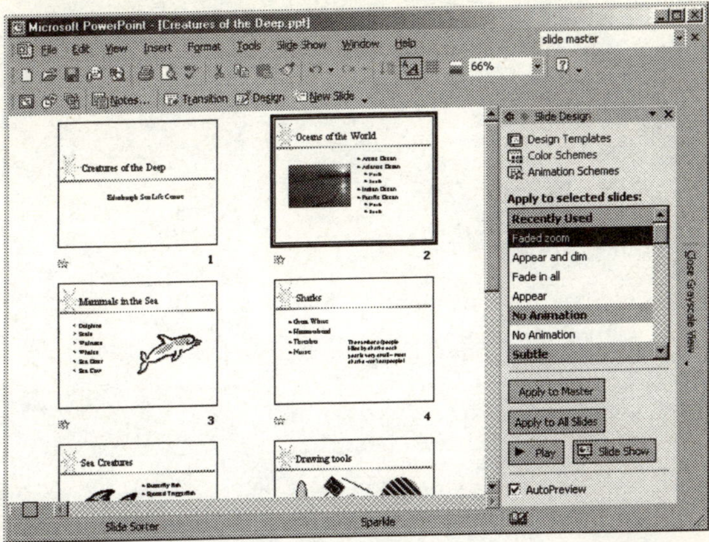

- With your slide selected in Slide Sorter view, click the Slide Show icon, work through your slide then press **[Esc]** to return to Slide Sorter view.

Custom animations

You can set up your own animations (rather than use the preset ones) if you wish. You must be in Normal view for this to work.

1 Go into **Normal view**

2 Display the slide that you wish to animate

3 Open the **Slide Show** menu and choose **Custom Animation**

4 Select the object on your slide that you wish to animate

5 Click the **Add Effect** button, and choose an effect from the options listed

6 Specify the **Start**, and other options – these vary depending on the effect chosen

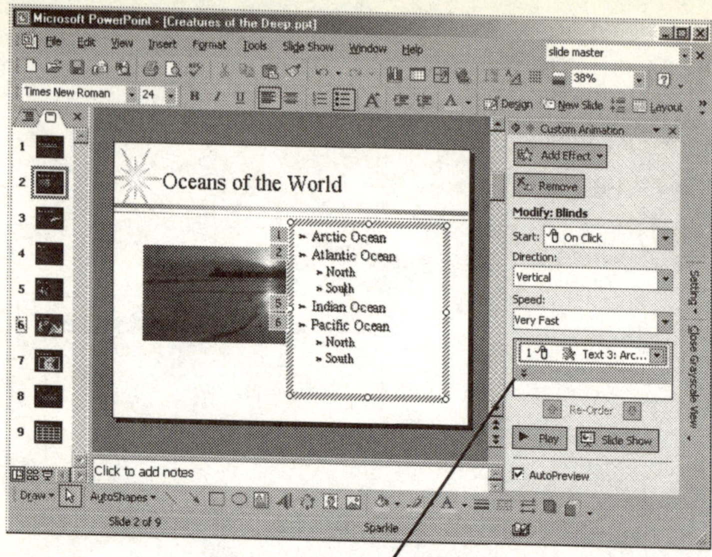

Click to see the list of items that have been animated. You can customize the animation for each item.

To customize the animation of an item:

1 Right-click on it in the list
2 Select **Effect Options**
3 Open the **Effect**, **Timing** or **Text Animation** tab
4 Specify the options
5 Click **OK**

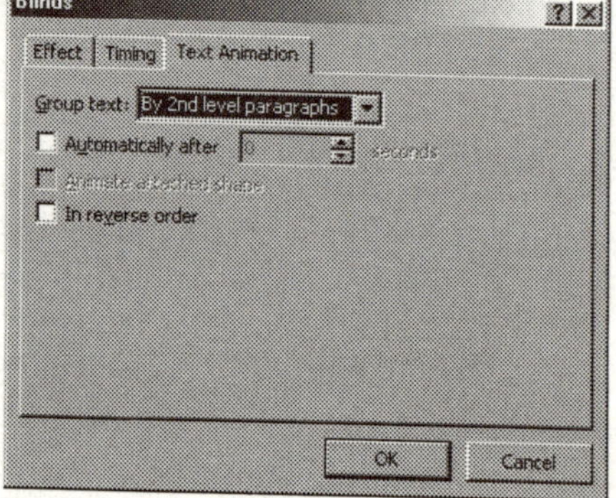

9.7 Set Up Show

A slide show can be presented in a number of different ways:

- By a presenter
- Driven by the audience
- Automatically

You may want to use all the slides in your presentation, or a sub-set of them.

You might want the slide show to run in a continuous loop, or you could choose to use or not use animation effects that you have set up.

The slides can be set to advance manually (when you click the mouse) or by using slide timings if you have saved them.

By default, a slide show is assumed to be presenter driven, with all slides used. Animation effects will run and the show will progress manually – when the presenter clicks the mouse.

However, if you wish your slide show to be controlled using either of the other methods (perhaps for an open day, or at a sales event), or if you wish to change any of the default settings, you can easily change the set up options.

To specify the slide show set up:

1 Open the **Slide Show** menu

2 Select **Set Up Show**

3 Specify the options required and click **OK**

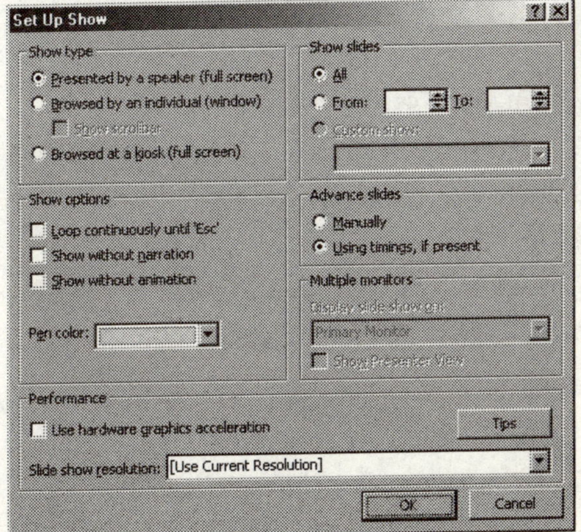

9.8 Custom Show

You can quickly set up a custom show from the slides that you have in your presentation if you wish. This could be useful if you have a number of slides in your presentation, but wish to be able to 'mix and match' them to different audiences.

To create a custom show:

1 Open the **Slide Show** menu
2 Choose **Custom Shows…**
3 Click **New…**
4 At the **Define Custom Show** dialog box, give your show a name

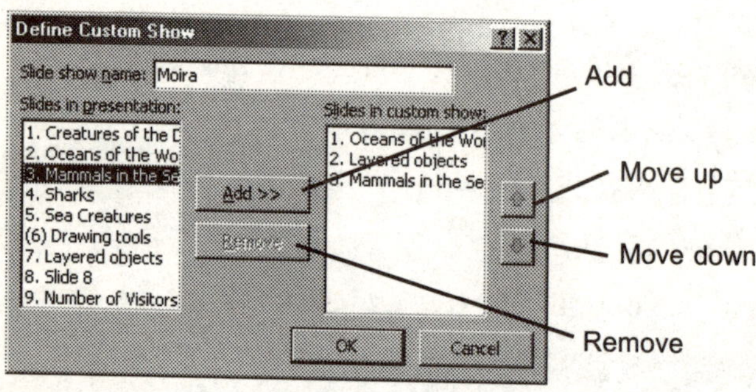

To add slides to the custom show:

1 Select the first slide you require from the list on the left
2 Click **Add** >> to add it to your show
3 Repeat until all slides have been added

To remove slides from the custom show:

1 Select the slide you wish to remove from the list on the right
2 Click **Remove**

To move slides within the custom show:

1 Select the slide you wish to move in the list on the right

2 Click the **Move Up** and **Move Down** button as necessary

When you are done, click **OK** to close the **Define Custom Show** dialog box, then click **Close** at the **Custom Shows** dialog box.

To edit a custom show:

1 Open the **Slide Show** menu
2 Choose **Custom Shows…**
3 Select the show that you wish to edit
4 Click **Edit…**
5 Add, remove or move slides as required
6 Click **OK**

To delete a custom show:

1 Open the **Slide Show** menu
2 Choose **Custom Shows…**
3 Select the show you wish to delete
4 Click **Remove**

To copy a custom show:

1 Open the **Slide Show** menu
2 Choose **Custom Shows…**
3 Select the show you wish to copy
4 Click **Copy**
5 Edit the copy as required

To show a custom show:

1 Open the **Slide Show** menu
2 Choose **Custom Shows…**
3 Select the show you wish to run
4 Click **Show**

Summary

In this chapter we have discussed some of the features that you can use to add the finishing touches to your presentation in preparation for your actual slide show.

We have looked at:

- Hiding slides that you may not want to use in your main presentation, but keep them easily accessible should you require them during the presentation
- Practising your presentation with the Rehearse Timings tool
- Adding a summary slide to your presentation
- Speaker Notes
- Adding Transitions to add impact as your slides appear during a slide show
- Animation schemes to gradually build up the main points on your slide
- The Set Up options for your slide show
- Creating Custom Shows

giving a slide show

In this chapter you will learn

- how to run your slide show
- some ways of working with your slide show
- how to build up minutes and action points during a show
- how to export minutes and action points to Word or Outlook

Aims of this chapter

In this chapter we will discuss the basic skills required to run a slide show, and some of the features that are available to you when delivering your presentation. These are useful when the presentation is presented by a speaker (rather than run automatically).

10.1 Slide Show

You can run a slide show at any time to check how the presentation is progressing. Each slide fills the whole of the screen. After the last, you are returned to the view you were in when you clicked the **Slide Show** tool.

1 Select the slide you want to start from, usually the first.
2 Click the **Slide Show** (from current slide) icon to the left of the horizontal scroll bar.
3 Press [**PageDown**] (or click the left mouse button) to move onto the next slide.

Press [**PageUp**] to move back to the previous slide if necessary.

- You can exit your slide show at any time by pressing the [**Esc**] key on your keyboard.
- Use the Slide Show together with Slide Sorter view when experimenting with Transition and Animation effects. Then you can check that the options you choose are having the desired effect.

Working within your slide show

When presenting your slide show, you might want to leave the normal sequence, go directly to a slide or draw on the slide to focus attention. These, and other features, can be accessed using the pop-up menu or the keyboard.

1 Click the pop-up menu icon at the bottom left of the screen, or right-click anywhere on the screen

To go directly to a slide:

2 Select **Go**, then **Slide Navigator**

3 Select the slide you want to go to

4 Click **OK**

Or

5 Select **Go**, then **By Title**

6 Click on the slide you want to go to

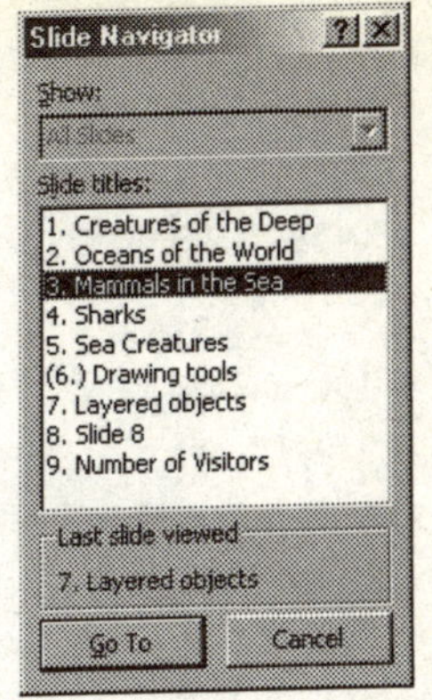

To run a Custom Show from a Slide Show:

1 Display the pop-up menu

2 Select **Go**, then **Custom Show**

3 Click on the show that you wish to run

To go back to the last slide that you viewed (not necessarily the previous slide in the presentation):

1 Display the pop-up menu

2 Select **Go**, then **Previously Viewed**

To go to a slide number:

1 Type the number of the slide you wish to go to

2 Press **[Enter]**

10.2 Blackout and whiteout

There are times when you might like to blackout or whiteout your screen so as not to distract your audience as you demonstrate or show them something.

To blackout your screen:

- Press **[B]**

To whiteout your screen:

- Press **[W]**

Press **[B]** or **[W]** again to return to your slide show.

Experiment with the pop-up menu to see what options are available.

Pens and arrows

You can change your mouse pointer to a *pen* so that you annotate a slide, or draw something on your 'blackboard' or 'whiteboard'.

To draw on your screen:

1 Press [Ctrl]-[P] to change the mouse pointer to a pen

2 Click and drag to draw

3 Press [Ctrl]-[A] to change the mouse pointer back to an arrow shape when you've finished.

To change the colour of your pen:

1 Right-click on your screen

2 Select **Pointer Options**

3 Choose **Pen Color**

4 Select the colour that you want to use

To erase your drawing:

- Press [E] on your keyboard

10.3 Meeting Minder

If you are using PowerPoint to give a presentation at a meeting, you may find Meeting Minder useful to help you generate your minutes.

As your presentation progresses, you can quickly access Meeting Minder to record any notes or action points.

To access Meeting Minder:

1 Right-click on a slide in the Slide Show

2 Select **Meeting Minder**

3 Record any notes that you wish to make on the **Meeting Minutes** tab

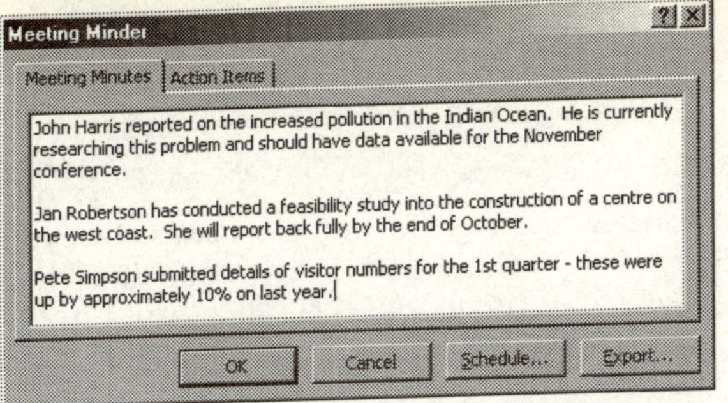

4 Record any actions on the **Action Items** tab, clicking **Add** after each item

5 Click **OK**

- To edit an item, select it, click **Edit**, update as necessary and then click **Add**
- To delete an item, select it and click **Delete**
- You can access your Microsoft Outlook Schedule from Meeting Minder by clicking **Schedule...**

Once you've finished your presentation, and your Meeting Minutes and Action Items have been added, you can export the data to Microsoft Outlook or Word (provided that you have them installed on your computer).

To export the data:

1 Click **Export...** in the **Meeting Minder** dialog box

2 Select the checkboxes as required

3 Click **Export Now**

Meeting Minder Export
Export options
Post action items to Microsoft Outlook
Send meeting minutes and action items to Microsoft Word
Export Now
Cancel

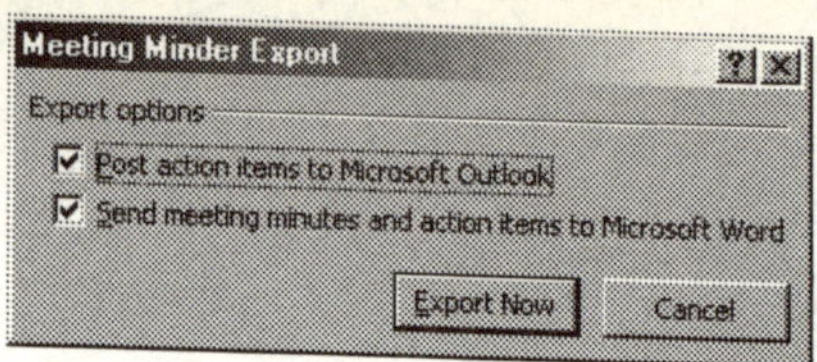

- Items exported to Outlook will be listed in your task list. You can edit them, or post them to someone from here
- Items sent to Word will be displayed in a Word document.

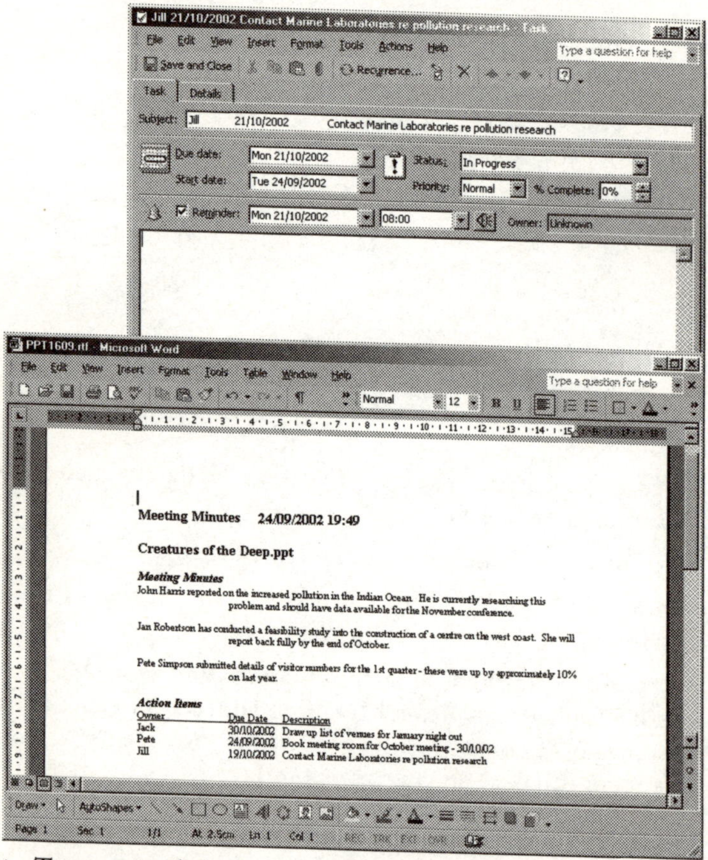

Jill 21/10/2002 Contact Marine Laboratories re pollution research - Task
File Edit View Insert Format Tools Actions Help
Type a question for help
Save and Close
Recurrence...
Task
Details
Subject: Jill 21/10/2002 Contact Marine Laboratories re pollution research
Due date: Mon 21/10/2002
Start date: Tue 24/09/2002
Status: In Progress
Priority: Normal
% Complete: 0%
Reminder: Mon 21/10/2002
08:00
Owner: Unknown
PPT1609.rtf - Microsoft Word
File Edit View Insert Format Tools Table Window Help
Type a question for help
Normal
12
Meeting Minutes 24/09/2002 19:49
Creatures of the Deep.ppt
Meeting Minutes
John Harris reported on the increased pollution in the Indian Ocean. He is currently researching this problem and should have data available for the November conference.
Jan Robertson has conducted a feasibility study into the construction of a centre on the west coast. She will report back fully by the end of October.
Pete Simpson submitted details of visitor numbers for the 1st quarter - these were up by approximately 10% on last year.
Action Items
Owner Due Date Description
Jack 30/10/2002 Draw up list of venues for January night out
Pete 24/09/2002 Book meeting room for October meeting - 30/10/02
Jill 19/10/2002 Contact Marine Laboratories re pollution research
Draw
AutoShapes
Page 1 Sec 1 1/1 At 2.5cm Ln 1 Col 1

- To get more help on the options available to you while running Slide Show, press [F1]. The **Slide Show Help** dialog box lists other options you might want to experiment with.

10.4 PowerPoint Show

You can save your PowerPoint Presentation (.ppt) file as a PowerPoint Show (.pps) file. When you open a PowerPoint Show file, you are immediately launched into Slide 1 of your show. When the show is over, the .pps file is closed again.

To save your .ppt file as a .pps file:

1 Open the presentation as usual
2 Choose **Save As...** from the **File** menu
3 Give your file a name (I suggest you use the same name as the .ppt file)
4 Choose **PowerPoint Show** as the file type
5 Click **Save**

To run your show from your .pps file:

1 Locate the file in either My Computer or Windows Explorer
2 Double-click on the filename

Summary

In this chapter we have considered:

- The skills needed to run your slide show
- Slide navigation during a show
- Running a Custom Show
- Slide show options, e.g. blackouts, whiteouts, pens and arrows
- Meeting Minder
- Slide Show Help
- Saving your presentation as a PowerPoint Show

printing presentations

In this chapter you will learn

- how to set up your presentation for printing
- how to specify what you want printed
- how to print a selection of slides

Aims of this chapter

This chapter discusses the print options available for your presentation. You can print your whole presentation in PowerPoint – the slides, speaker notes, audience handouts and the presentation outline. You can print copies of your slides onto paper or onto overhead transparencies, or you could get a bureau to create the slides for you.

11.1 Page setup

The first stage to printing your presentation is to specify the slide setup. You set the slide size and orientation at this stage.

1 Choose **Page Setup** from the **File** menu
2 Select the size from the **Slides sized for** field
3 Specify the orientation required for the **Slides**
4 Specify the orientation required for the **Notes, handouts & outline**
5 Click **OK**

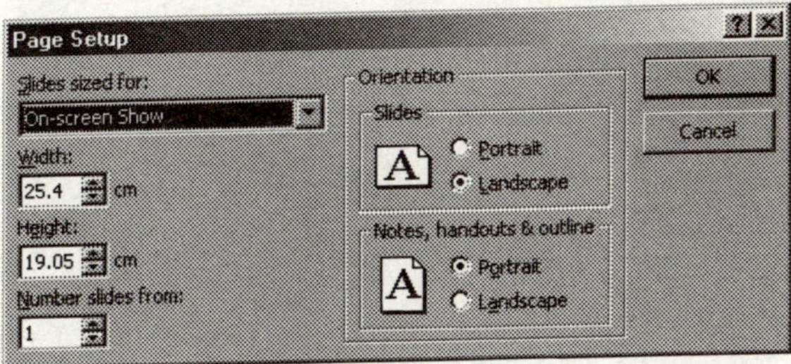

- All slides in a presentation file must be in one orientation – either landscape or portrait. If you wish to combine slides of different orientations in the same slide show, you could use hyperlinks to link separate presentation files.

The next table summarizes the main options in the **Slide sized for** list (you can check the others out in the list yourself).

Type	Width	Height	Notes
On-screen show	25.4 cm	19 cm	Orientation to Landscape; 3:4 aspect ratio
Letter paper	25.4 cm	19 cm	3:4 aspect ratio
A4 paper	27.5 cm	19 cm	Aspect ratio between that of on-screen show and 35 mm slides
35mm slides	28.5cm	19 cm	Content will fill the slide in landscape orientation 2:3 aspect ratio
Overhead	25.4 cm	19 cm	Select for overhead transparencies
Banner	20.3 cm	2.54 cm	
Custom			Set own measurements

- If you change the slide orientation, you may find that you need to change the size and shape of placeholders on the Slide Master to get your objects to fit well.

Letter paper size, portrait orientation.

11.2 Printing slides

With the Page Setup details specified for the output required, you can go ahead and print your slides. I recommend that you preview your presentation before you print it. If you do not like the preview, adjust as necssary and preview again, until you are happy that it is ready for printing.

To preview your presentation:

- Click the **Preview** tool on the Standard toolbar, or open the **File** menu and choose **Preview**

The Preview toolbar is displayed with your slide.

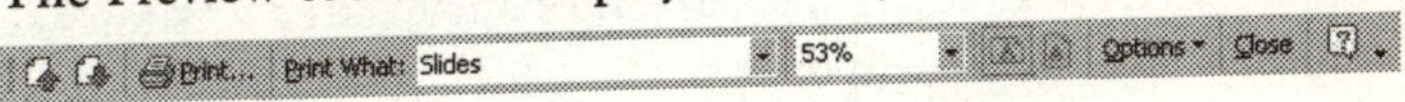

Take a look at the Preview toolbar. From left to right you have:

- **Previous Page**
- **Next Page**
- **Print…** displays the **Print** dialog box
- **Print What:** choose from slides, handouts, notes or outline
- **Zoom** – the default option fits the slide/page on the screen. You can increase or decrease it if you wish

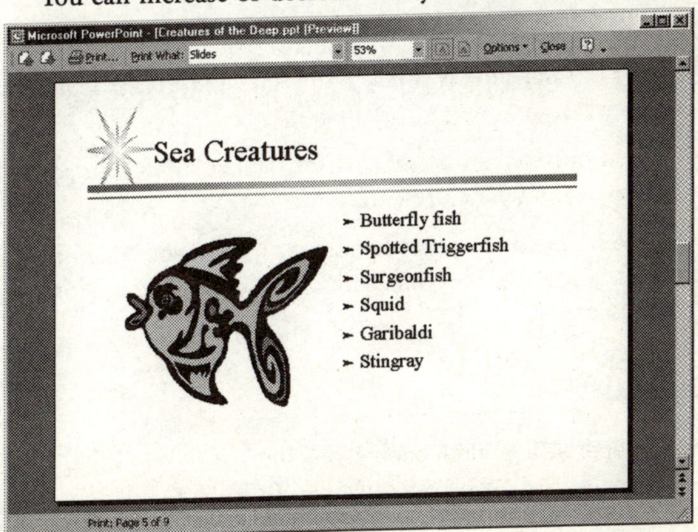

- **Landscape** or **Portrait** – orientation options available for handouts, notes pages and outline
- **Options** – further options to choose from (see next page)
- **Close** – closes the preview window

Print What:

Slides

Prints onto paper or overhead transparencies, one slide per page.

Handouts

You can print miniatures of your slides out to issue as audience handouts – 1, 2, 3, 4, 6 or 9 to the page.

Printing your handouts with 3 slides to the page is particularly useful as there is room for your audience to make their own notes. The 9 slides per page option is a good way to get a summary for your own use.

Notes Pages

A slide miniature is printed, together with any notes that you have made to prompt you during your presentation.

Outline

The text of each slide is printed out, showing the structure of the presentation.

A printed outline can be very useful in that it lets you see an overview of the whole presentation.

When you choose to print handouts, notes pages or outline, the orientation tools become active so you can specify Portrait or Landscape.

Options

Other print options are available in the Options list. Some of the options are also available in the Print dialog box.

Header and Footer

Displays the Header and Footer dialog box (see 8.2).

Color/Grayscale

This option allows printing in Color, Grayscale or Pure Black and White. The Grayscale and Pure black and white print options are useful for printing notes pages and handouts. The following table gives guidelines on how some of the objects print in grayscale and in pure black and white.

Object	Grayscale	Pure black and white
Text	Black	Black
Text shadows	Hidden	Hidden
Embossing	Hidden	Hidden
Fills	Grayscale	White
Frame	Black	Black
Pattern fills	Grayscale	White
Lines	Black	Black
Object shadows	Grayscale	Black
Slide backgrounds	White	White
Charts	Grayscale	Grayscale

You can also choose to view your slide in Grayscale or Pure black and white in Normal view – the Color/Grayscale tool is on the Standard toolbar.

To change the appearance of objects in Grayscale and Pure black and white in Normal View:

1 Right-click on your slide
2 Choose **Grayscale Setting** or **Black and White Setting**
3 Select an option

Scale to Fit paper

This option automatically scales your slide to fit the paper size.

Frame Slides

Toggles a slide border, or frame, on or off.

Print Hidden Slides

Prints slides that have been marked as Hidden (see 9.1) as well as those that have not.

Include Comment Pages

Prints out the comments sheet for any slide that has a comment on it.

Print Order

Allows you to specify whether the slides are printed down the page then across, or across the page then down (handouts).

- If you click the print icon on the standard toolbar, one copy of each slide is printed. To print anything else you must go into Print Preview or access the **Print** dialog box and specify what you want to print in the **Print what:** field.

11.4 Print dialog box

Many of the options that can be specified in Print Preview, can also be specified in the **Print** dialog box.

You can display the **Print** dialog box by using **File > Print**, or by clicking **Print...** on the Print Preview toolbar.

Print selection

If you don't want to print out all of your slides, you can specify which ones you do want in either Slide Sorter view or in the **Print** dialog box.

In Slide Sorter view:

1 Select the slides you wish to print in Slide Sorter view (click on the first one, then [Ctrl]-click on each additional slide)

2 Open the **File** menu and choose **Print...**

3 Choose **Selection**

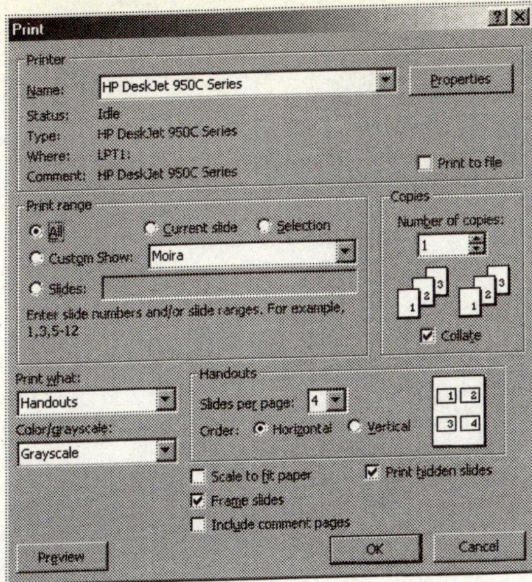

In the Print dialog box:

1 Specify the slides that you wish to print in the **Slides** field

- Click **Preview** in the **Print** dialog box to preview your work before you print it.
- If you are going to send your slides to a service bureau to be turned into 35mm slides or other materials, contact the bureau for any specific information on file formats required.

Summary

This chapter has introduced some of the printing facilities that are available in PowerPoint. Areas covered were:

- Page Setup options for slides, notes, handouts and outline
- The Print Preview tools and printing options
- The Print dialog box
- Printing selected slides – from Slide Sorter view and from the Print dialog box

jumps and links

In this chapter you will learn

- how to use Action Buttons
- how to add text and sound
- how to combine landscape and portrait slides
- how to add a hyperlink to an object

Aims of this chapter

In this chapter we will look at Action Buttons. These are found in the AutoShapes list on the Drawing toolbar. You can use the them to jump from one place to another in a presentation, or to link through to another presentation, file or program. The Action Buttons can be added to any slide you wish – they become activated when you are running your slide show on a computer.

12.1 Action buttons

To add an Action Button to a slide:

1 Display the slide on which you want to put an Action Button

2 Choose **Action Buttons** from the **AutoShapes** list

3 Select a button

4 Click where you want the button to appear

5 Complete the **Action Settings** dialog box

6 Click **OK**

7 Resize or reposition the Action Button if necessary

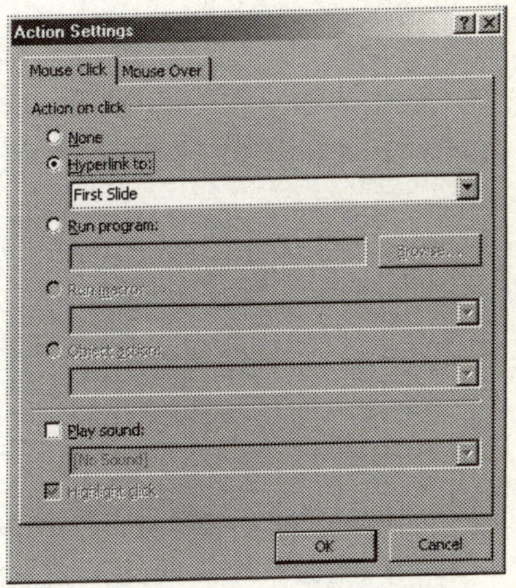

- If you like adding Action Buttons to your slides, make the **Action Buttons** submenu a floating menu (drag its title bar) – to give you quick access to all the buttons. You can dock the menu at the top, bottom, right or left of your screen.

The Action Buttons toolbar

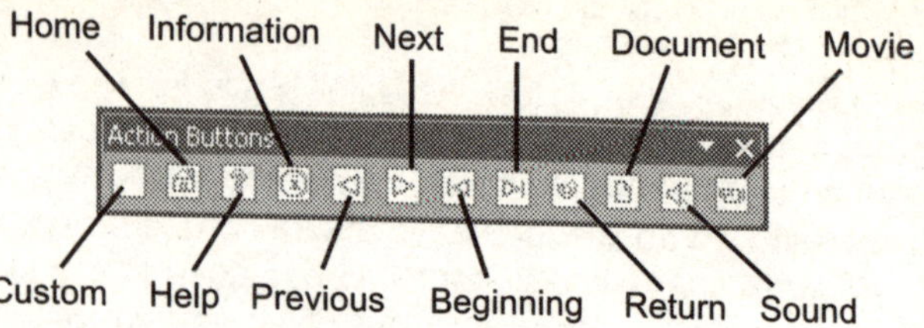

Action Button Settings

Most of the Action Buttons have default settings – you can easily change these in the **Action Settings** dialog box.

To edit the settings of an existing Action Button:

1. Right-click on the button
2. Choose **Action Settings** from the shortcut menu
3. Select the **Mouse Click** or **Mouse Over** tab
4. Specify the settings required
5. Click **OK**

Adding sound to your Action Button

You could add a sound to your action button – the sound will play when the Action Button is clicked, or when the mouse moves over it.

1. Right-click on the button
2. Choose **Action Settings** from the shortcut menu
3. Select the **Mouse Click** or **Mouse Over** tab
4. Click the **Play Sound** checkbox
5. Select a sound from the list available

Or

6. Click **Other sound…** at the bottom of the list
7. Browse through your folders until you find more sound files (there are several in C:\Windows\Media)

8 Select the file required in the **Add Sound** dialog box

9 Click **OK**

10 Click **OK** at the **Action Settings** dialog box

You can add text to any Action Button, although it is probably most likely that you will add text to the Custom button as it contains no image.

To add text to an Action Button:

1 Right-click on the button

2 Select **Add text** from the menu

3 Enter the text into the text box

4 Click anywhere on your slide

- Action buttons are activated when you give a slide show.

You can link through to any other PowerPoint Presentation file and slide using this technique.

12.2 Mixed slide orientation

In any PowerPoint file, the orientation is either landscape (the default) or portrait. You can't have some of the slides landscape and some portrait in the same file. If you want a presentation with slides in both orientations, Action Buttons and hyperlinks can help. You need to set up two files – one with the orientation landscape and the other portrait. You can then use Action Buttons to link one presentation to the other when required.

To link from one presentation file to another:

1 Set up your main presentation file – leaving out any slides that are in the other orientation, e.g. landscape

2 Set up a second file with the remaining slides – with the other slide orientation set, e.g. portrait

3 In the main presentation file, place an Action Button on the slide that precedes a slide from the second file – I suggest you use the **Custom** button

4 In **Hyperlink to:** choose **Other PowerPoint Presentation**
5 Select the file that contains the other slide(s) and click **OK**
6 Specify the slide you want to jump to
7 Click **OK** to close the **Hyperlink to Slide** dialog box
8 Click **OK** to close the **Action Settings** dialog box

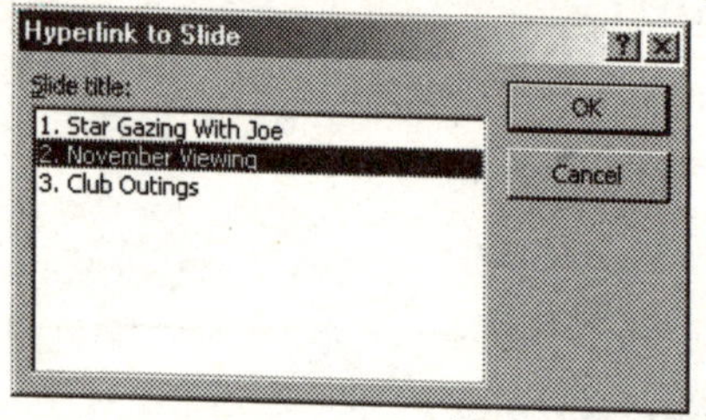

To switch between files during a slide show:

1 Click the Action Button to jump to the second file when you reach the appropriate slide
2 View the slides in the second file, using the usual techniques to move from slide to slide as necessary
3 To return to the main presentation file, press [Esc]. The **Slide Show** toolbar will appear – select **Resume Slide Show**

12.3 Hyperlink from any object

You don't have to use Action Buttons to hyperlink to different places in your file, to another file or to an Internet address.

You can attach a hyperlink to most objects – Text, AutoShape, clip art, WordArt, etc.

To attach a hyperlink to an object:

1 Select the object you want to hyperlink from

Or

- Place the insertion point within the word you want to hyperlink from

2 Click the **Insert Hyperlink** tool

3 Type the path or browse for the file you want to link to – it could be on your disk, on your company Intranet or on the Internet

4 Click **OK**

- During a slide show, you can jump to the hyperlink using your chosen method – either Mouse Click or Mouse Over.
- When you jump to a hyperlinked file, click the **Back** tool on the Web toolbar to return to your presentation.

Summary

In this chapter we have discussed:

- Adding Action Buttons to slides
- Editing Action Buttons settings
- Adding sounds to Action Buttons
- Using Action Buttons to link presentation files to produce slide shows with mixed slide orientation
- Adding hyperlinks to objects on your slides

13 toolbars

In this chapter you will learn

- some tricks for working with toolbars
- how to add, remove and move tools on toolbars
- how to create a new toolbar

Aims of this chapter

In this chapter we discuss toolbars. We'll look at basic toolbar manipulation – the positioning of toolbars on the screen and showing and hiding toolbars. We'll also discuss how you can edit existing toolbars, create new toolbars and assign macros to toolbars.

13.1 Showing and hiding toolbars

You may have noticed that some toolbars appear and disappear automatically as you work in PowerPoint. The Picture toolbar appears when a clip art object is selected, the WordArt toolbar appears when a WordArt object is selected.

You can opt to show or hide toolbars whenever you want.

Provided you have at least one toolbar displayed, you can use the shortcut method to show or hide any toolbar.

To use the shortcut method:

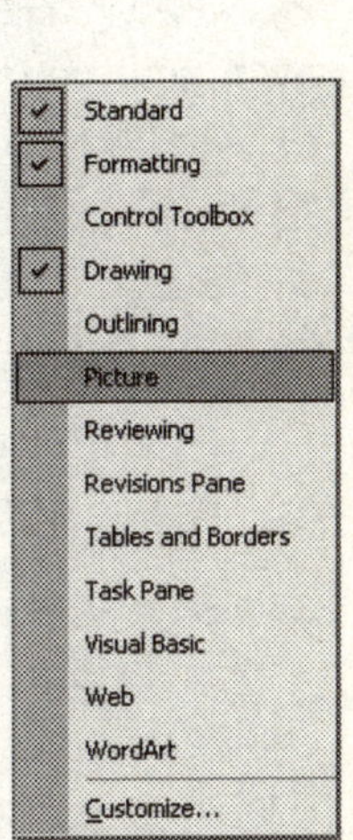

1 Right-click on a toolbar

- Any toolbars that are displayed have a tick beside their name, any that are not displayed have no tick.

2 Click (using the *left* mouse button) on the toolbar name you wish to show or hide

If no toolbars are displayed, you must use the **View** menu to show them again.

1 Open the **View** menu and choose **Toolbars**

2 Click on the one you want to show

Using either method, you can show or hide one toolbar at a time. If you want to change the display status of several toolbars at once, it may be quicker to use the **Customize** dialog box.

1 Right-click on any toolbar

Or

- Open the **View** menu and choose **Toolbars**

Or

- Click the drop-down arrow at the right of a toolbar and choose **Add or Remove Buttons**

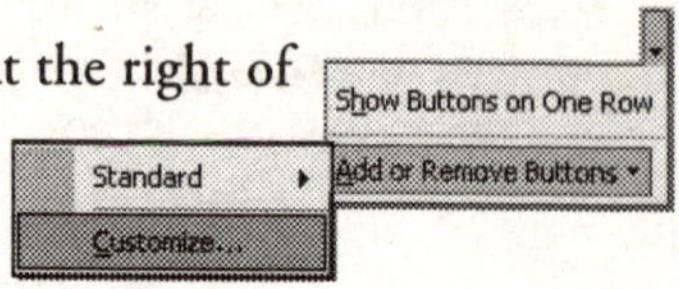

2 Click **Customize...**

3 On the **Toolbars** tab, select or deselect the toolbars in the list as required (a tick means they are displayed, no tick means they are hidden)

4 Click **Close**

13.2 Moving toolbars

Toolbars can be positioned *anywhere* on your screen. There are four *docking* areas – at the top, bottom, left and right of your screen, and your toolbars can be placed in any of them. You can also leave your toolbar floating in the document area if you prefer.

The Standard and Formatting toolbars are normally displayed along the top of your screen, side by side, sharing one row.

To move a toolbar:

If the toolbar is docked

1 Point to the two raised lines at the left edge of the toolbar (if it is docked at the top or bottom of the screen) or top edge (if it is docked at the left or right)

2 Drag and drop the toolbar to the position you want it in

If the toolbar is not docked

1 Point to its Title bar

2 Drag and drop the toolbar into its new position

If you don't want the Standard and Formatting toolbar to share one row, you can switch off this option. The Standard and Formatting toolbars can then be positioned as they were in previous versions of PowerPoint – the Standard one above the Formatting one.

To disable the row-sharing option:

1 Click the drop-down arrow at the right of the Standard or Formatting toolbar

2 Choose **Show Buttons on One Row** or **Show Buttons on Two Rows** as required

13.3 Editing existing toolbars

When you first start to use PowerPoint, the toolbars display the tools that perform some of the most regularly used functions, e.g. new presentation, open, save, print. As you work with PowerPoint, the toolbars are customized automatically to display the tools that you have used most recently.

Automatic customization of toolbars:

1 Click the drop-down arrow at the right of a toolbar

2 Select the tool required from those displayed

- The tool will be placed on the displayed area of the toolbar so that you can access it again quickly

Adding and removing tools

If you find that there are some tools on a toolbar that you tend not to use, or if you want to add another tool to a toolbar, you can easily add or remove tools. If you want to add several tools to a toolbar, you should create a new toolbar and add your tools to it – see 13.4 below. If you want to edit a toolbar it must be displayed.

1 Click the drop-down arrow to the right of the toolbar that you wish to edit

2 Click **Add or Remove** buttons

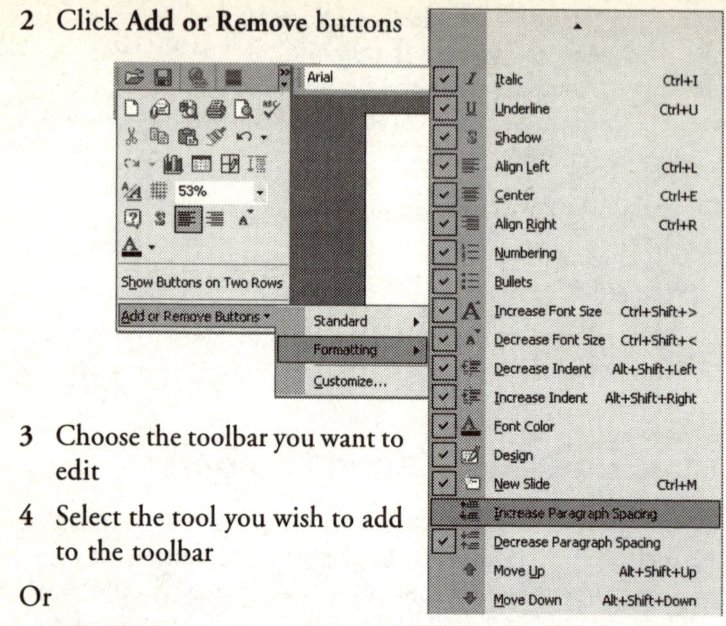

3 Choose the toolbar you want to edit

4 Select the tool you wish to add to the toolbar

Or

- Deselect the tool you wish to remove from the toolbar

5 Click in the presentation

To edit an existing toolbar from the Customize dialog box:

1 Right-click on a toolbar that is currently displayed

Or

- Open the **View** menu and choose **Toolbars**

Or

- Click the drop-down arrow at the right of a toolbar and choose **Add or Remove Buttons**

2 Click **Customize...**

3 Select the **Commands** tab

To add a tool:

1 Select the **Category** of tool you're looking for

2 Locate the command you require from the **Commands:** list

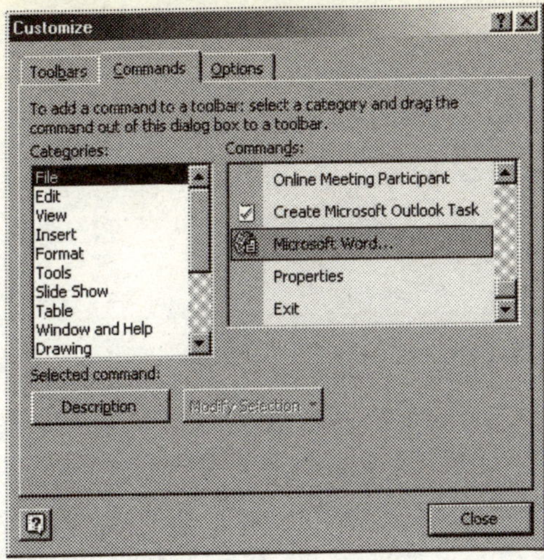

3 Drag it over to the toolbar. When you are over a toolbar a very dark I-beam with a + beside it indicates your position. Drop it in the position required (if you are not over a toolbar, the mouse pointer has a small button with an **x**)

If you want a brief description of a tool's purpose, select it in the list of commands on the **Commands** tab, or on the toolbar, then click the **Description** button.

To move a tool:

1 Drag the tool to its new position on the toolbar

2 Drop it

To remove a tool:

1 Drag the tool off the toolbar

2 Drop it anywhere

- Click **Close** when you've finished editing your toolbar.

The drop-down lists that appear on toolbars, e.g. Style box and Font box on the Formatting toolbar take up a lot more room than one of the picture tools.

If you need to make a bit more space on a toolbar that contains drop-down tools, you can change their size as required.

To change the size of a drop-down tool, you must have the **Customize** dialog box open.

1 Select the tool you want to resize, e.g. Arial
2 Click and drag the right or left edge of it – the mouse pointer becomes a thick double-headed arrow ↔ when you are in the correct place

Shortcut

You can quickly move or delete tools from a toolbar that is displayed *without* opening the Customize dialog box.

To move a tool:

Hold down the [Alt] key and drag it along the toolbar (or to another toolbar)

To delete a tool:

Hold down the [Alt] key and drag it off the toolbar

13.4 Reset toolbar

If you have edited a PowerPoint toolbar, then decide that you want to reset it, you can easily do so. The toolbar will return to how it was when you installed PowerPoint.

To reset your toolbar:

1 Open the **Customize** dialog box
2 Display the **Toolbars** tab
3 Select the toolbar you wish to reset
4 Click the **Reset…** button
5 Click **OK** at the prompt

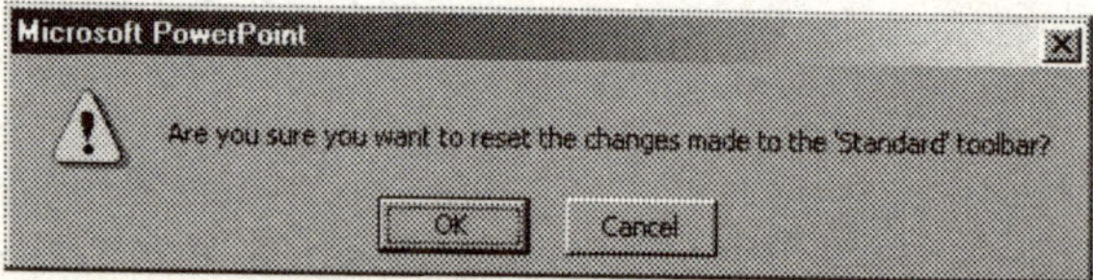

13.5 Creating a new toolbar

If you want to add several tools to a toolbar, you may find that you need to create a new toolbar, rather than try to squeeze tools into the existing ones.

To create a new toolbar:

1 Right-click on a toolbar that is currently displayed

Or

- Open the **View** menu and choose **Toolbars**

Or

- Click the drop-down arrow at the right of a toolbar and choose **Add or Remove Buttons**

2 Click **Customize…**

3 Select the **Toolbars** tab

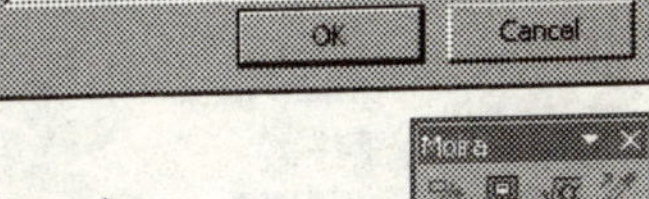

4 Click **New…**

5 Give your toolbar a name and click **OK**

6 Your new toolbar will be displayed

7 Choose the **Commands** tab and add the tools you require

8 Close the **Customize** dialog box

Summary

In this chapter we have discussed the various options available when working with and modifying toolbars:

- Positioning toolbars on your screen
- Showing and hiding toolbars
- Adding tools to toolbars
- Moving tools on toolbars
- Removing tools from toolbars
- Creating new toolbars

In this chapter you will learn

- what linking and embedding mean
- how to use PowerPoint with Excel
- about creating PowerPoint presentations from Word and Word documents from PowerPoint presentations

Aims of this chapter

PowerPoint is part of the Microsoft Office suite, and it integrates very well with the other applications in the suite. If you have installed the complete Office suite then you have the benefit of being able to use the best tool for the job. This chapter discusses some of the ways in which the Office applications can be integrated.

14.1 Linking vs embedding

Linking and *embedding* are two techniques that enable you to incorporate data from other applications into your PowerPoint document. The main difference between linked and embedded data lie in:

- Where it is stored;
- How it is updated.

Linked data

Linked data is not stored in your PowerPoint presentation. It is stored in a file, e.g. a workbook or document, in the source application (the one it was created in). The data is updated within the source application – and those changes are reflected in the PowerPoint presentation to which it is linked.

Features of linked data include:

- The PowerPoint presentation is smaller than it otherwise would have been.
- The data in the presentation reflects the current status of the source data.

Embedded data

Embedded data is stored in your PowerPoint presentation. However, when you create and edit the data, you have access to all the functions within the source application.

Features of embedded data:

- All the data is held in one document.
- You have access to powerful functions that are not part of PowerPoint when creating and editing the object.

The following sections discuss some of the methods you can use to integrate the data across the applications in Office.

- Section 14.2 discusses simple copy and paste techniques to get data from one application to another.
- Section 14.3 discusses Paste Special (this option enables you to link the data in one application to another).
- Section 14.4 discusses converting Word documents to PowerPoint presentations, and vice versa.

14.2 Copy and paste

You can copy text, data, graphics, charts, etc. from one application to another within the Office suite using simple copy and paste techniques.

To copy and paste:

1. Launch PowerPoint and the application you want to copy from
2. Select the object, text or data you want to copy
3. Click the **Copy** tool on the Standard toolbar
4. Switch to PowerPoint and display the slide you want to paste on to
5. Place the insertion point where you want the object, text or data to appear
6. Click the **Paste** tool on the Standard toolbar

Data pasted in from Excel or Access is displayed in a PowerPoint table, and can be edited and manipulated using PowerPoint's table-handling features. Text copied from Word is placed in a text box.

When you copy data using this method, it is not linked to the original data in Excel, Access or Word in any way. Should you edit the data in the source application, the data you copied into PowerPoint remains as it was when you copied it.

14.3 Copy and Paste Special

If you want the data that you copy into your PowerPoint document to be kept in line with the data held in the source application, you should create a link to it. You must use Copy and Paste Special to create a link.

You can use Paste Special to link to files in Excel or PowerPoint.

To create a link to data or a chart in Excel:

1 Open the workbook that contains the data or chart you want to create a link to
2 Select the data or chart required
3 Click the **Copy** tool
4 Switch to PowerPoint
5 Open the presentation, and display the slide that you want to paste into
6 Open the **Edit** menu and choose **Paste Special...**
7 Select the **Paste Link** button

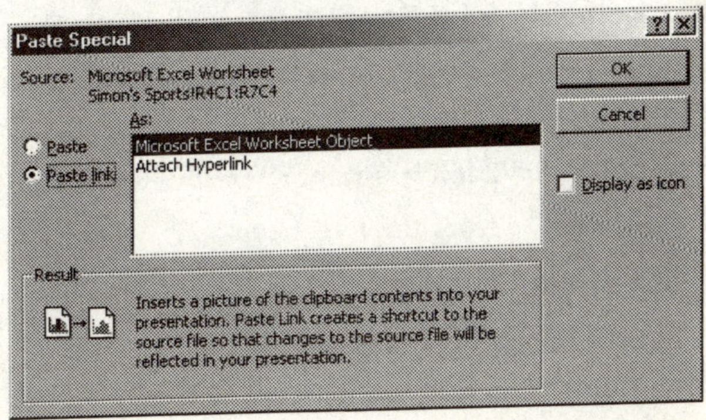

8 Choose an option from the **As:** list – when you select an option a brief description of how it works appears in the **Result** box

9 Click **OK**

14.4 PowerPoint and Word

In addition to Copy and Paste or Paste Special techniques, there are other ways of working between PowerPoint and Word.

PowerPoint presentation from Word documents

You can quickly create a PowerPoint presentation from a Word document. The Word document must be set up as an outline (see Word online Help), and you must format the text in your Word document using the heading styles 1-9 as PowerPoint uses the heading levels to structure the slides it creates. Text formatted using the *Heading 1* style in your Word document will be used for the slide title on each new slide, *Heading 2* styles will be used as the first level of bullet points, etc.

To create the presentation:

1 Open your Word document if necessary

2 Choose **Send To** from the **File** menu

3 Click **Microsoft PowerPoint**

Word documents from PowerPoint presentations

You can also quickly generate a Word document from a PowerPoint presentation.

1 Open the presentation you want to create a document from

2 Choose **Send To** from the **File** menu

3 Select **Microsoft Word**

4 Choose a page layout and paste option

5 Click **OK**

A new document will be created in Word. You can save and/or print the document as required.

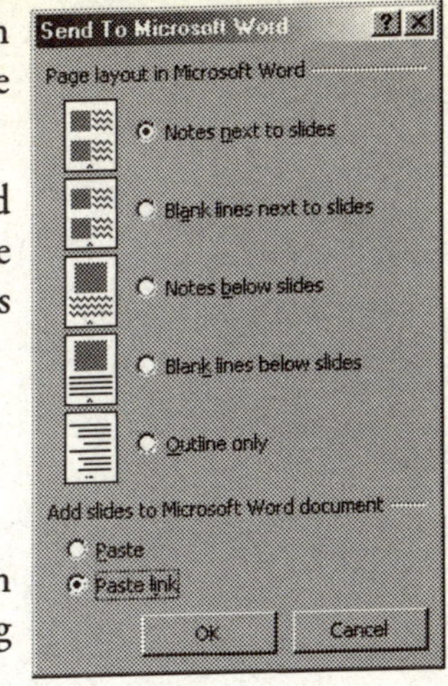

If you opt to Paste link, your Word document will automatically update when the PowerPoint presentation is edited and saved.

Meeting Minder

See section 10.3 for information on exporting data from Meeting Minder to Word or Outlook.

Summary

In this chapter we have discussed some of the ways you can integrate PowerPoint with the rest of the Microsoft Office suite. We have discussed:

- Linking and Embedding
- Copy and Paste
- Copy and Paste Special from Excel and Access
- Creating a PowerPoint presentation from a Word document
- Creating a Word document from a PowerPoint presentation

taking it further

If you've mastered half of what's in this book, you are well on the way to becoming a proficient PowerPoint user. If you are getting to grips with most of it, you are doing very well indeed.

You'll find lots of information on PowerPoint on the Internet, in addition to the Help menu option Office on the Web that takes you to http://office.microsoft.com/uk/assistance/.

Other sites that you may find useful include:

http://www.microsoft.com/office/powerpoint/default.asp

http://search.support.microsoft.com/search/

You could also try searching the Web for sites that provide information on PowerPoint. Try entering "*Microsoft PowerPoint*" + "*Software Reviews*" into your search engine. You should come up with several sites worth a look.

If you would like to join a course to consolidate your skills, you could try your local college, or search the Internet for on-line courses. Most courses cost money, but you may find the odd free one – try searching for *+PowerPoint +Tutorial +Free*.

Good PowerPoint skills are useful on many different levels – personal, educational and vocational. Now that you have improved your PowerPoint skills, why not consider going for certification? The challenge of an exam can be fun, and a recognized certificate may improve your job prospects. There are a number of different bodies that you could consider.

You may want to consider MOUS exams (Microsoft Office User Specialist) or ECDL (European Computer Driving Licence) certification. Or, if you feel more ambitious, how about other Microsoft Certified Professional exams!

Visit **http://www.microsoft.com/traincert/mcp/mous/** for information on MOUS certification or **http://www.ecdl.com** for information on ECDL.

index

Action Buttons 131
Action Buttons toolbar 132
Alignment 34
Animation
  in organization charts 74
  on slides 108
Application title bar 6
Arrows, in a slide show 118
AutoContent Wizard 22
AutoShapes 48

Blackout 117
Blank Presentation 20
Boxes, on organization charts 72
Bullet points
  indent level 35
  moving 36
Bullets
  customized 38
  pictures 40

Category axis, chart 58
Chart objects 61
  formatting 62
Chart Type 59
  custom 60
Charts 55
  combination 64
  importing from Excel 65
Clip art 86
  formatting 91
Clip Organizer 87
Clips online 90
Color/Grayscale print options 127
Column widths in charts 64
Comments 41
Copy and paste 146
Curve Autoshape 48
Custom animations 109
Custom Show 112
  running 117

Datasheet 57
  hiding rows and columns 59
Design Template 21
  changing 40
Diagram Gallery 69
Diagrams 77
  adding shapes 79
  changing layout 80
  creating 78
  types 79
Distribute Rows/Columns 85
Docking areas 138
Drawing tools 46
Drawing toolbar 6, 44

Embedded data 145
Exiting 16

Flip 49
Font formatting 33
Formatting text 33
Formatting toolbar 6, 58
Freeform Autoshape 48

Getting into PowerPoint 5
Graphs 55
Group 51

Handout Master 99
  editing 100
Handouts 2
  printing 126
Hardware and software requirements 3
Headers and Footers 99
Help 8
  Ask a question box 9
  Contents Tab 12
  Dialog Box 15
  Index Tab 13
  Office Assistant 9
  Office Assistant, customize 10
  on the Internet 15
  Screen Tips 14
  Tips 11
  What's This? 11
Hide Slide 103
Hide/Restore panes 28
Hyperlinks 133

Indents, promoting/demoting 35
Installation 4

Keyboard shortcuts 34, 35
Keywords, for clip art 89

Legend 62
Linked data 145

Master Layout 98
Master View 96
Media Clip 93
Meeting Minder 118
  exporting data 119
Menu bar 6
Menus 7
  using the keyboard 8
  using the mouse 8
Menus and toolbars
  personalizing 7
Microsoft Graph 56

Normal view 25
Notes Master 100
Notes Page view 25
Notes Pages, printing 126
Notes Pane 6, 27
Number formats 58
Numbering 37

Objects 4
  formatting 47
  Group and Ungroup 51
  layers 50
  rotate and flip 49
  working with 44
Open presentation 25
Organization chart 69
  animation 74
  autoformat 74
  formatting 73
  layout 73
  toolbar 70
Orientation 123
Outline 3
  printing 126
Outline and Slides pane 26
Outline tab 26

Page setup 123
Paste Special 147
Pens, in a slide show 118
Picture toolbar 91
Picture formatting tools 92
Pictures, selecting 86
Placeholders 19, 98
PowerPoint and Word 148
PowerPoint Show (.pps) file format 121
PowerPoint window 6
Presentation 3
Presentation graphics 2
Presentation pane 6
Presentations
  closing 24
  new 19
  opening 25
  saving 23
Preserve Master 97
Preview toolbar 125

Print dialog box 128
Print What: options 126
Printing slides 125
Rehearse timings 104
Rotate 49

Save As 24
Scale 63
Scale to Fit, print option 127
Set Up Show 110
Shapes in diagrams 79
Slide layout, changing 40
Slide Master 96
  new 97
Slide Master View toolbar 99
Slide Navigator 117
Slide orientation 124
Slide Show 116
  Slide navigator 117
Slide Show view 26
Slide Sorter toolbar 103
Slide Sorter view 26, 103
Slides 2
  adding 31
  deleting 32
  moving and copying 32
  printing 126
Slides and Outline tabs 6
Slides sized for 123
Slides tab 27
Sound 93
Speaker Notes 2 106
Standard toolbar 6, 57
Starting 5
Status Bar 6
Summary Slide 106
Symbols 39

Tables 83
  drawing 84
  working with 85
Tables and Borders toolbar 83
Task Pane 6, 20
  New Presentation 19
  Slide Design 20, 40
  Slide Layout 20, 55
  Slide Transition 106
Text formatting 33
Text box 45
Text object 44
Timings
  displaying 105
  Rehearse 104
Title Master 96
  new 97
Toolbar
  Action Buttons 132
  Drawing 6, 44
  Formatting 6
  Organization Chart 70
  Picture 91
  Preview 125
  Show/hide 137
  Slide Master View 99
  Slide Sorter 103
  Standard 6
  Tables and Borders 83
  WordArt 52
Toolbars
  creating 143
  customizing 140
  editing 139
  modifying 139
  moving 138
  row-sharing 7
Tools
  adding and removing 140
Transitions 107
Transparent color, clip art 93

Undo 45

Value axis, chart 58
View icons 6
View options 25
View/hide datasheet 58

Whiteout 117
WordArt 52
WordArt toolbar 52

Zoom 25